HOT
COUNTRIES

W9-AZB-747

ALEC WAUGH

has also written

❧

NOVELS:

THE LOOM OF YOUTH

THE LONELY UNICORN

CARDCASTLE

KEPT

LOVE IN THESE DAYS

NOR MANY WATERS

THREE SCORE AND TEN

SHORT STORIES:

PLEASURE

THE LAST CHUKKA

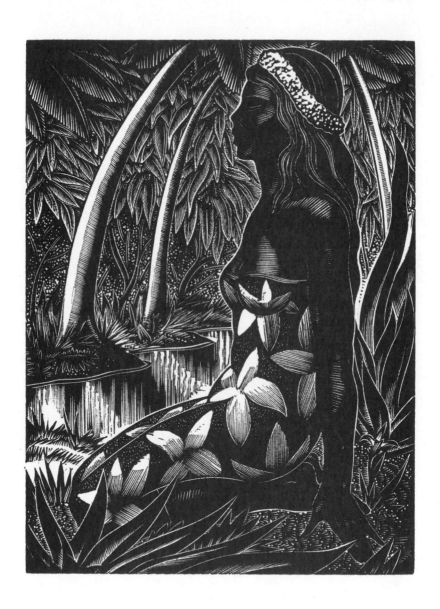

HOT COUNTRIES

by

ALEC WAUGH

Wood Engravings by Lynd Ward

PARAGON HOUSE • NEW YORK

First paperback edition, 1989

Published in the United States by

Paragon House
90 Fifth Avenue
New York, NY 10011

Copyright © 1930 by Alec Waugh
Copyright © renewed 1958 by Alec Waugh

Library of Congress Cataloging-in-Publication Data

Waugh, Alec, 1898-1985
  Hot countries / by Alec Waugh ; with woodcuts by Lynd Ward. — 1st
pbk. ed.
     p.   cm.
  Reprint. Previously published: New York : Farrar & Rinehart, c1930.
  Includes index.
  ISBN 1-55778-209-1
  1. Tropics.   2. Voyages and travels.   3. Waugh, Alec. 1898-1985.
I. Title.
G905.W38   1989
828'.91203—dc19   88-30128
                                                                  CIP

Manufactured in the United States of America

CONTENTS

CONTENTS

viii

HOT
COUNTRIES

AT SEA

I

"The first question to ask about a travel book," I have heard it said, "is, can the author go back to the places he has described?" Usually he can't. Those books that are more than bread and butter letters addressed to the people from whom their author has received hospitality, have not brought the novelist into good repute. I have noticed at times a quizzical look in the eyes of the officials and planters to whom I have been introduced.

"What, another of you fellows coming here to write us up?"

Well, that is not a thing that I have ever done. I have never gone to a place to write it up. I have travelled for the sake of travel. Novel writing has this advantage over most other jobs, that your office premises are portable. During the last few years I have covered a good many miles, calling in at the places where I have friends or that

I have felt curious about, carrying on with my job of story-telling in cabins and hotel bedrooms, mingling as I should in London with the life that I have found about me.

And if you travel in that way you cannot write exhaustively of subjects. This book is a narrative of personal impressions. It is like casual fireside talk when the stream of anecdote and reminiscence carries you from sea to sea, from continent to continent. Penang reminds you of Tahiti, Dominica of the Siamese teak forests; Haiti recalls the mosquito-hung lagoons of the New Hebrides. I have written as I have travelled. My plan has been to have no plan.

§

It began, I suppose, in the spring of 1925, with the reading of *The Trembling of a Leaf*. I was staying at Diano Marina with G. B. Stern, and through an entire evening Geoffrey Holdsworth and I discussed *The Fall of Edward Barnard*, the story of a young Chicagoan who leaves America with the intention of making a fortune in the South Seas, only to surrender his ambition in an atmosphere of soft glances and soft airs. For three hours we discussed the problem of the "beachcomber." Why, we asked ourselves, should man work himself in a cold inequitable climate towards an early grave when so little a while away livelihood lay ready to his hand? Why make life difficult when it might be easy? Why avoid a sunlit leisure? Did it really profit a man that he should make fortunes in Lombard Street when copra can be sold at a few francs a bag on the palm-fringed edge of a lagoon?

That started it. For on my return to London, a fort-

2

night later, I was met by Petre Mais' exuberant curiosity.

"Now what's all this I hear from Geoffrey Holdsworth about you and the South Sea Islands?"

I stared blankly. What, indeed?

"I hear," he went on, "that you and he sit up all night discussing them, and that you've made up your mind to settle there."

"Hardly that."

"You'ld like to, though."

"If there's a place," I said, "where one can live on thirty thousand words a year, it's well worth while having a look at it."

Next morning the readers of the *Daily Graphic* were informed that on the previous day Mr. Londoner had lunched with Mr. Alec Waugh, who could talk about nothing except the South Sea Islands, which he was planning to tour shortly. That settled it. The snippet is the only part of a newspaper that is really read. You can have your novel noticed in reviews of a column's length, in paper after paper, and only such of your friends as have received a presentation copy of it will be aware that it is out. On the other hand, the inclusion of your name in the list of guests at a raided night club is certain to be seen by everyone. There is no limit to the power of the paragraph. It is the one part of a morning's paper that is not dead by lunch-time. As the Buddhists conceive immortality, it is immortal. It dies but it is re-born. It is the candle from which lamps are lit. During the next few weeks every mention of me in the press referred to a Mr. Waugh, who was shortly to desert London for the

3

South Sea Islands. I found myself included in leaderettes on "The Lure of the Pacific." Men came up to me in my club with a "Look here, about this trip of yours . . ." I heard so much talk about the Islands that I had to buy an atlas to find out where Tahiti was.

To begin with, it was amusing. Later on it became embarrassing. I felt as Tartarin did when his brave talk of lions was taken literally. And as the weeks passed and nothing happened, I found as Tartarin found, that I was being regarded with suspicion. People seemed surprised and a little indignant at meeting me still in London. "What, not gone yet?" they said. I felt that I had no right to be in Piccadilly, that I was a gate crasher who had better go before he was turned out. Precipitately, I flung myself upon the cares of the Western Shipping Agency.

"I want," I said, "to go round the world."

By the time I had got back I had developed the travel habit.

And it is not easy to break oneself of habits. Once, after two years of almost continuous wandering, I vowed that never again would I set foot upon a liner. I was weary of packing and unpacking, of state-rooms and cabin trunks. I longed for the amenities of a compactom wardrobe, of bookshelves and arm-chairs. For twenty-four months I seemed to have done nothing but fill and empty drawers. "Never again," I told myself as I signed a seven years' lease for a flat in Chelsea. I meant it too. At thirty, I thought, one should begin to think of settling down. But within three months that flat was in the hands of the house agents and I was suggesting to Eldred Curwen that he should desert Europe and a Ballot for Martinique

4

and a canoe. Once again my trunk was covered with the French Line's red and yellow labels.

§

When I was a prisoner of war in Germany, supporting life upon a daily ration of three slices of bread, five bowls of watery soup, and six potatoes, I could not believe that the day would ever come when I should rise from a table on which food remained. In much the same spirit, as the *Pellerin de Latouche* steamed up the Garonne towards a Biscay that was to justify its reputation, I could not believe that on this actual boat within a week's time we should be panting beneath electric fans in unbuttoned shirts, clamorous for open windows.

It was clearly, for the first days, anyhow, to be an unpleasant voyage. The ship was crowded. The sea was rough. And I am not one of those happy travellers who love the ocean in all its moods. A storm at sea is, I am sure, a noble spectacle. The beating of the wind upon one's face, the dashing of the waves across the deck, the spray turned into a rainbow by the sun, the quivering of the ship as trough after trough of waves is breasted; it is all, I am very certain, very fine. But it is rather differently that I have seen it.

Ignobly prostrate in my cabin, I have watched through half-seeing eyes my possessions heap themselves into chaos on the floor. As a Victorian moralist watched during the War the overthrow of beliefs that he had looked on as immutably fixed loadstars, so have I watched objects that in harbour had seemed part of a permanently ordered

5

scheme of living, sway, shiver and disappear. As the curtains over porthole and door swung inwards I have watched my wardrobe, garment by garment, detach itself from hook and hanger. I have watched my combs and brushes, my links and studs and shoe-horn slither over the polished surface of the dressing-table. I have watched gramophone records skate majestically towards the floor, to mingle with shoes and suit-cases in a measured sliding from one side of the cabin to the other, in time with the lurching ship. I have heard the crash of cabin trunks; have listened hour by hour to the rattle of a tooth-glass against a mug; have listened and have not cared.

Nor can I honestly confess to any sense of shame. On my second morning I made a gallant, rather than a judicious, appearance in the dining-room. And a careful scrutiny of the depleted tables left me unconvinced that it is to the highest of his creatures that the Lord has granted immunity from sickness.

It was not a particularly pleasant trip. I am doubtful whether any really long sea voyage is.

At the start it is fun enough. There is a real kick to that first walk round the ship that for three weeks or a month is to be your home; that is to contain all you are to know of friendship, boredom, interest, romance. You scan surreptitiously, with an eager curiosity, the faces of your fellow passengers. Soon enough they will reveal themselves as the familiar types. Before lunch-time on the third day you will know who it is that is going to make speeches and propose healths in the dining saloon, whose voice it is that will harry you with shouts of "Red lies two. Good shot, partner, oh, good shot!" You will recognise those with whom you are likely to become friends and those between yourself and whom you will be at pains that there shall always be the length of half a deck. In forty-eight hours you will know them all. But for the moment they are mysterious and unknown. They are like an unopened mail. There is a spring in your stride as you stroll along the deck. You have been at trouble that the impression you are yourself to make shall be as good as possible. Your tie has been carefully chosen. You are wearing your happiest suit.

But the sense of novelty is soon lost, and when it is once lost the passing of each day seems very long. Life develops into an attempt to find an antidote to boredom. Each nationality has its own medicine. The French employ a policy of passive non-resistance. Everyone does nothing resolutely. You rise late in pyjamas, to loll about the deck till the hour before lunch when you go below to shave and change. After lunch you siesta. After tea you read. As soon as possible after dinner you go to bed. The English are aggressive. Every instant of the day must be employed. There are sports committees and concert committees and fancy-dress committees, and at every odd moment of the day harassed secretaries are chasing you round the deck to tell you that you must be ready to play your heat in the deck quoits in five minutes' time. The Americans settle down to bridge in the smoking-room directly after breakfast, and do not leave it except for meals till the bar is closed at midnight. I do not know which method is the best. For a six days' trip I prefer the American. But after a week one's liver resents the strain. For ten days deck games may be amusing, but ten days are the limit. After that, one is exhausted and involved in a dozen feuds. Whereas the French method, though it prohibits all social intercourse and is devastating for a short voyage—I recall in particular a voyage between Colombo and Singapore when literally I spoke to only one man and only to him at meals—is the only attitude that I can imagine possible on a long voyage, since it does not force people into such close contact with each other that they get immediately upon each other's nerves. But even so, however one takes it, the experience of a long voyage is an exacting one.

The trip on the *Pellerin* was no exception. I was counting seconds, not hours, by the tenth day out of Plymouth. And yet when the last night came, on this, as on every other trip that I have ever taken, I found myself limply surrendering to the conventional sentimental wistfulness.

§

I have read much and seen a little of the genuine pathos of last nights on board when the brief but deep friendships of a fortnight's passage are sundered in all human probability for ever. But on the *Pellerin*, such contacts as had come to us had been superficial. Yet all the same, as the last day closed and the sudden tropic night with its train of unfamiliar stars swept statelily over the calming waters, Eldred and I found ourselves growing sad and silent.

What was it? The surrender simply to a facile uprush of obvious emotions? "We never," said De Quincey, "do anything consciously for the last time without regret." Like trees we take root where we are planted. And I fancy

8

that our instinctive sadness at these moments of uprooting is something more than a false idealising of the past simply because it is the past; that the psychologist would detect in it a recognition subconsciously of the symbol in our brief sojourning of the sojourning only relatively less brief of all mortality; that in this loss of things and faces that have grown familiar we are abandoning a series of amulets, of reassurances in a continuity that possibly does not exist; that this sudden last hour friendliness for a number of persons with whom we have little if anything in common and whose acquaintance, were it made in the customary routine of life, we should never bother to follow up, is based upon genuine sentiment.

It may be. But be it how it may, the phenomenon remains that whether the voyage has been long or short, grey or pleasant; whether its end is to mean the opening of a new and entrancing chapter of fresh experience, or a return made grudgingly to conditions from which we can only temporarily escape; always there rises on that last night a clouded mood of melancholia. People to whom you have scarcely spoken during the voyage come up to you after dinner, "What, going to-morrow?" they say. "That's sad. We shall be a less cheerful party."

And you sit talking, not as you have talked on other evenings, casually, without enthusiasm because your eyes were too tired for the reading you would have preferred, but eagerly, intimately, expansively, in quick, coloured sentences, in a desperate haste to get said in this short night all that must otherwise remain unsaid. And right through the conversation will run motif-wise the refrain. "How tragic that this should be our last night."

9

It is ridiculous, but there it is.

For days Eldred and I had been counting the hours to our release. For days we had been telling ourselves that neither in this nor any other life did we wish to see again one inch of those sulky sea-splashed decks, or one foot of all the feet that had trodden them. Yet when the time had come for us to drift quietly through the still waters of the Caribbean we were almost regretting that on the next night it was to be under the grey shadow of Carbet that we should be sleeping.

§

It was wet and misty as the *Pellerin de Latouche* drew into Fort de France, and it was hard to distinguish the lettering on the large, broad-beamed cargo flying a French flag, that followed us into dock. There was, however, a familiar quality about that long, low ship with its single funnel, its black airholes, its squat, white superstructure; and yet I could scarcely believe that chance should have brought into that harbour at that moment a ship that only three times in a year and for a few hours touched there. It would be the kind of coincidence that the novelist is counselled to avoid scrupulously. And yet it was very like the ship that twenty-four months before I had seen steam slowly into the Segond Channel.

I turned to the Commissaire.

"What's that boat over on our right?" I asked.

"That," he answered. "Oh, that's the *Louqsor*."

He spoke rather contemptuously. And no doubt the *Louqsor* to the Commissaire of an ocean liner would seem a somewhat discreditable acquaintance. To describe her as a cargo boat is to say nothing. The word cargo boat evokes a picture of Kipling's "black bilboa tramp," and a "drunken dago crew." But nowadays there are not too many such. The smartest small ship I ever travelled on was the *Handicap*, a Norwegian cargo boat running between Europe and Seattle, that I boarded as she was passing through the Canal. She was an oil burner of 9,000 tons. There was never a speck of dirt upon her. The crew were housed in small, clean, airy cabins; two or three men in each. The twenty-three days' journey to London was the most comfortable I have ever had. She carried no passengers—I had to sign on as an assistant purser. My cabin was large and cool, the food better and more varied than I should have had on any save a transatlantic liner. There was naturally no saloon. But the captain, a married man, travelling with his wife and two small children, had the kind of flat for which, furnished, you would pay four guineas a week in London. The word "cargo" boat nowadays means simply "not carrying passengers."

Indeed, by that criterion, cargo is an inexact description of the *Louqsor*. It does carry passengers, a few. Built twenty-five years ago as a troopship, it now runs on the Messageries intermediate service between Noumea and Dunkerque. It is an old-fashioned ship. The steering apparatus is arranged on the outside, so that all night long a chain is rattling outside your cabin porthole. There is no cold storage, so that your meat has to be carried fresh. The front part of the ship is like a farmyard. There are sheep and bullocks and pigs and chickens. You feel as though you were travelling on the Ark. The great feature of the ship's life is the slaughter, twice weekly, of a bullock; a spectacle for which most of the passengers and any available deck hands assemble. The cabins are not large, the dining saloon is also the smoking-room, the bar, the library, and the music-room. When it rains there is no part of the deck on to which water does not leak. There is no promenade deck. If you want to take exercise, you have to take it between barrels of kerosene and wine on an unawninged deck. There are only two baths, one for women, the other for the male passengers and officers. It is not the kind of ship that a tourist agency would charter, but of the thirty or so ships on which I have travelled during the last four years it is by a long way my favourite.

Romance and glamour are bound up with it. From its decks I saw for the first time the mountains of Tahiti. With its engines throbbing, six months later I set out from Marseilles for the long voyage southwards and westwards through Panama to the Pacific. But it is not for these things alone I love her. I have known no ship where the life on board is more personal, familiar, sympathetic; where one feels more at home; where everyone on the ship, sailors, white and black, passengers, saloon and steerage, gives the impression of belonging to one family. There is a delightfully free and easy atmosphere. You sit about in pyjamas all the morning; you stand on the bridge watching the slow swaying of the prow as she cuts her way through the blue waters. When we crossed the equator the entire ship was devoted to aquatic revelry. Sailors and passengers chased each other with hose pipes and buckets of water along every deck. And yet in spite of this casual atmosphere discipline is never relaxed. The captain remained dignified and reserved, the master of his ship. As, indeed, all French captains do. We are told often that the French are indifferent sailors. They may be. That I am unable to judge. But this I do know: that their captains in the merchant service compare very favourably with the British ones. Most of my travelling has been done on French boats, on the boats of the C.G.T., and the Messageries Maritimes. I have scarcely ever travelled on a first-class English liner—the Atlantic ferry boats are hotels rather than ships—but on the smaller liners there is an unfortunate tendency among British captains to consider as their chief concern the entertainment of their passengers. They behave as though they were the conductors of a pierrot troupe. That I have never seen happen on a French ship.

On the *Louqsor* life followed a calm routine. One woke with the sun at six. There was a leisurely dressing and *petit déjeuner*. By half-past seven I was in a corner of the dining saloon, a pen in hand, with four hours of work ahead of me. We lunched at eleven-thirty. At twenty past twelve the clock was put back to twelve. Through the heavy heat of the day we siestaed in long canvas chairs, sleeping a little, talking a little, reading desultorily. From five to half-past six I took my exercise on the lower deck; a solitary walk, through which I planned my next day's writing. After dinner there was nothing to do but to sit out on deck listening to a gramophone. Not an exciting life, but the most harmonious atmosphere I have ever known at sea. When I saw the *Louqsor* limping away towards Moorea, I felt—it is a clichéd phrase but there is no other adequate—that it was taking something of my-self away with it. I never expected to see its weather-beaten prow again.

It was an extraordinary coincidence that its arrival in Fort de France should have coincided with my own. Not the most extraordinary that I have known. The most extraordinary happened in the spring of 1928, when P. T. Eckersley, the Lancashire cricketer, was on the *Berengaria* with me, on his way to the West Indies for a cricket tour. It was a be-galed and be-fogged journey. On the first day out of Cherbourg the seas were so heavy that the engines were slowed down. We reached the Hudson River six hours late, to find an impenetrable mist laid low upon it. For two days we were marooned. A melancholy two days in prohibition waters. For every one it was a dismal time. But for no one was it more exasperating than for Peter Eckersley. The connection he had meant to make in New York would be lost. It would be a week before another boat would sail. He would be late for the first Test Match. Gloomily he paced the unvibrating decks.

And then just about tea-time, on the second day, there was a faint quiver through the ship. Everyone ran to the taff-rail to see, feet below it seemed, a ship that had col-lided with us. It was a seven or eight thousand ton affair, but it looked an absurd midget alongside the majestic *Berengaria*. It was a David assaulting a Goliath. We mocked it as the Philistines mocked David, when suddenly Eckersley gave a gasp.

"Good heavens! I believe that's the ship I should be on," he cried. It was; the ship that should have taken him to the West Indies and the first Test Match, that he had no chance of catching now, lay alongside of us thirty feet below. In his cabin were his trunk and cricket bag. He had only to lower them over the side and follow after. Yet there he had to sit waiting for the mist to rise, for the midget steamer and the vast liner to drift apart, for the *Berengaria* to move westward to the bleak climate of New York, and the little fruit boat to the sunlight and the palm trees and the level fields.

That, I think, was the most curious coincidence I have ever known. But the episode of the *Louqsor* was a quaint one. So quaint that I half wondered whether the arrival at the same hour as myself of this ship with which, in one way or another, is bound up most of what in the last three years has mattered personally to me, was not an omen, a symbolic beckoning back of me towards Tahiti. On the top of the gangway there was the black notice board, "Le *Louqsor* partira pour Colon à neuf heures." And in five days' time the word Colon would have been rubbed out, the word Papeete substituted. In five days' time. And three weeks later there would be the jagged outline of the Diadem.

We dined that night with Alec Daunes, the second captain, and his brother-in-law; the only two officers who had not changed since I had made the trip. And all the time we talked about Tahiti.

"There's nothing like it," Daunes insisted. "I've been at sea for twenty years. I've seen most parts of the world, east and west. But if I were left two thousand dollars a year I'ld go to Tahiti, and as long as I lived never ask anything else of life." Then, persuasively, "Why not come

15

on with us to-morrow? You've not got your trunks un-
packed yet. Why not come?"

It was tempting; more than tempting when we were
back on the ship for a last drink before we said good-bye.
It was hard to believe, when we were grouped round the
familiar table in the familiar cabin, that I had ever left,
that I could ever leave, that ship.

"Come on now," they pleaded. "We'll send one of the
men back to the hotel to fetch your trunks. Stay on
here. It'll be so simple. When you wake up next morning, we'll be out of sight of land."

It was very tempting. And Eldred, I believe, was ready
enough to yield. I resisted, though.

"Tahiti. I've said good-bye to it, I think, for ever."

Which, two years back, was the last thing that I could
ever have imagined myself saying.

TAHITI

II

I SHALL never forget my first sight of Tahiti. For months
I had been planning to go there. For weeks I had been
dreaming of going there. But on the eve of my arrival I
craved for one thing only: a magic carpet that would
carry me to London. I had been travelling for eight
months and I was very tired: tired of new places and new
settings. My ears were confused with strange accents and
my eyes with changing landscapes. To begin with there
had been the Mediterranean. Naples, Athens, Constantinople. A few hours in each. A hurried rushing to the
sights: then the parched seaboard of the Levant. Smyrna
with its broken streets, and hidden among its ruins the
oasis now and then of a shaded square where you can drink
thick black coffee beside fat Syrians who puff lazily at
immense glass-bowled pipes. Smyrna and Jaffa and Bey-
rout. An island or two. The climbing streets of Rhodes,

17

the barren ramparts of Famagusta. Then Egypt and the
mud houses. And the tall sails drifting down the Nile.
Then Suez and the torment of the Red Sea when the heat
is so intense that perversely you long to be burnt more and
at lunch eat the hottest of hot pickles neat, till the inside
of your mouth is raw: a torment that lapses suddenly
into the cool of the Indian Ocean.

There had been Ceylon. The Temple of the Tooth at
Kandy, with its scarlet and yellow Buddhas so garish and
yet so oddly moving, as though there had passed into
those pensive features something of the brooding faith of
the hands that chiselled them; and the lake at Kandy after
dusk, when the fireflies are thick about the trees; and the
streets of Kandy on the night of the Perihera, when gilt-
shod elephants lumber in the wake of guttering torches.

And afterwards there had been Siam. Bangkok with
its innumerable bright-tiled temples and the sluggish
waterways that no hand has mapped; those dark mysterious canals, their edges crowded with huddled shacks,
their surface ruffled by the cool, slow-moving barges in
which whole families are born, grow up, see love and life
and die. Siam and the jungles of the north through which
I trekked day after day, slithering through muddied paddy
fields, climbing the narrow bullock tracks that cross the
mountain. There had been Malaya, green and steaming
when the light lies level on the rice fields; and Penang
where I had lingered, held by the ease and friendliness of
that friendly island, cancelling passage after passage till
finally I had had no alternative but to cancel the visit I had
planned to Borneo.

"I'll spend a month in Sydney," I had thought. "Then

I'll push on to the Pacific." But I had been away six
months before I left Singapore, and each place that I had
been to had meant the forming of new contacts and relationships, the adapting of myself to new conditions.
And as the *Marella* swung into Sydney Harbour and I saw
lined up on Circular Quay a smiling-faced crowd of relatives and friends, that sudden sensation of nostalgia which
is familiar to most travellers overcame me. England was
at the other side of the world. I was lonely and among
strangers. That very afternoon I was enquiring at the
Messageries about the next sailing for Noumea. And as a
month later the *Louqsor* rolled its way eastward through
the New Hebrides, I lay back in my hammock chair upon
the deck, a novel fallen forward upon my knees, dreaming
not of the green island to which each day the flag on the
map drew close, but of the London that was waiting a
couple of months away.

And then I saw Tahiti.

But how at this late day is one to describe the haunting
appeal of that island which so many pens, so many brushes
have depicted? The South Seas are terribly *vieux jeu*.
They have been so written about and painted. Long before you get to them you know precisely what you are
to find. There have been Maugham and Loti and Stevenson and Brooke. There is no need now to travel ten thousand miles to know how the grass runs down to the lagoon
and the green and scarlet tent of the *flamboyant* shadows
the road along the harbour; nor how the jagged peaks of
the Diadem tower above the lazy township of Papeete; and
beyond the reef, across ten miles of water, the miracle that
is Moorea changes hour by hour its aureole of lights. And

there has been Gauguin; so that when you drive out into the districts past Papara through that long sequence of haphazard gardens where the bougainvillea and the hibiscus drift lazily over the wooden bungalows, and you see laid out along their mats on the verandahs the dark-skinned brooding women of Taravao, their black hair falling down to their knees over the white and red of the *pareo* that is about their hips, you cry with a gasp of recognition, "But this is Gauguin. Before ever I came I knew all this." Everything about the islands is *vieux jeu*. And yet all the same they get you.

For that is the miracle of Tahiti, as it is the miracle of love—for though you have had every symptom of love catalogued and described, love when it comes has the effect on you of something that has never happened in the world before—that the first sight of those jagged mountains should even now touch in Stevenson's phrase "a virginity of sense."

Spell is the only word that can describe adequately that effect. Tahiti is beautiful, but no more beautiful than many islands—Penang, Sicily, Martinique—that touch the heart certainly, but far faintlier. There are no fine houses and no ample roadways. For the most part the sand is black, so that scarcely anywhere do you find those marvellous effects of colour, those minglings of greens and blues and purples that will hold you entranced for a whole morning in Antigua. There is no reason why, when you sit at dusk on the balcony of Moufat's restaurant, you should have that sensation which only and on occasions supreme beauty stirs in you of being in tune with the eternal. For it is upon a dingy square that you are looking down, nor would the *arrivist* care to be recognised in Bond Street in any of the dilapidated cars that are drawn round it. And it is the backs of houses—grubby affairs of wood and corrugated iron—that are on your right, and to the left there are the meaner of the Chinese stores; dingy, ill-lit, with bales of crudely printed cloths, and imitation silk, and the tawdrier of Indian shawls. There is not a single object for your eye to rest on that possesses the least intrinsic artistic value. Yet there are those who would rather dine on the rickety balcony at Moufat's than see the Acropolis by moonlight.

You can fall in love at first sight with a place as with a person. And I had fallen in love with Tahiti before ever I had set foot in it.

As the ship swung slowly through the gap in the reef I could see the children bathing in the harbour. There was a canoe drifting lazily in the lagoon. The quay was crowded with half the population of Papeete. They were laughing and chattering and they waved their hands. As the ship was moored against the wharf and the gangway was let down, a score or so of girls in bright print dresses, with wreaths of flowers about their necks, some quarter white, some full Tahitian, scrambled up the narrow stairway to welcome their old friends among the crew. The deck that had been for a fortnight the bleak barrack of an asylum became suddenly a summered garden. The spirit of Polynesia was about it, the spirit of unreflecting happiness that makes the girls wear flowers behind their ears, and the young people smile at you as you pass them by, and the children run into the roadway to shake your hand.

It was in a tranced state that I walked past the little group of trading schooners to where the tables at the Mariposa Café were filling up. It was five o'clock, the hour at which the offices and the stores are closed. The waterfront was crowded with people returning from their work. It was a variegated crowd. There were the Frenchmen, smart and dapper in their sun helmets and white suits. The Tahitian boys with narrow-brimmed straw hats. The island girls barefooted, in long print dresses that reached halfway down their calves, their black hair flung loose about their shoulders or gathered high with a comb upon their heads. They wore, most of them, behind their ears the white flower of the *tiare*. They walked with strong, swinging, upright stride, while beside them and among them, dainty in frocks that had been copied from Californian fashion plates, were the *blondes* and *demi-blondes*, some of them pushing bicycles, others loitering in the shadow of a parasol.

A variegated crowd, a mingling of every nationality and race. Yet they gave the impression of belonging to one family. For that is another of Tahiti's miracles: that it cancels all differences of race and caste. In the old days, when it was the custom among the Polynesians to exchange their babies, there grew up a saying that they were all brothers and sisters on the islands, since no one knew for a surety who was the child of whom. And now, though the custom is dying or has died, its influence persists in the feeling of kinship that binds together this variously blended, variously conditioned race.

On the verandah of the Mariposa Café, at the next table to mine, there were seated some half dozen girls who

were chattering merrily and noisily together. When I
ordered a cocktail they burst into a roar of laughter.

"Cocktail," cried one of them. "So that's your middle
name? Mine's rum."

For a moment I was puzzled, wondering into what odd
menagerie I had landed. But before we had exchanged five
phrases I had realised that their greeting implied no more
than friendliness: that introductions were an unnecessary
inconvenience on the island.

"When we like the look of any one," they said, "we
speak. What's your phrase, Tania?"

"A feeling is a feeling."

And they all burst into a roar of laughter.

They were always laughing, for no reason in particular,
out of sheer lightheartedness. And I brought my chair
over to their table. And we chattered away in a rapid
mixture of French, English and Tahitian in which French,
being the only language which we could all speak with
any fluency, predominated.

"And you're sailing on the *Louqsor?*" they asked.

I supposed I was.

Ah, but I wasn't to, they protested. We could have
such fun together. They would take me out into the
districts and we would eat *feis,* which is the wild banana,
because no one who had eaten *feis* could leave Tahiti. And
as I sat at ease and happy among those happy people, while
the sun sank, a mist of gold-shot lilac, behind the crested
outline of Moorea, I felt that my life would be half-lived
were I to sail five days later.

How I was to avoid sailing, however, I did not see. I
have rarely been more penniless than I was at that mo-

ment. All my life has been passed upon a shoe string. The moment that money comes to me I spend it. Overdrafts and account rendered bills are the framework of my existence. I live, have lived, and expect to die in debt. But this time I had not only been improvident, I had been unfortunate. Just as the *Marella* was leaving Singapore I received a telegram from London with the news that the chief commercial concern on which my livelihood depended had gone into liquidation and the residue of emoluments long overdue was being farmed parsimoniously by the public receiver. Had I received the news a day earlier I should have returned to England. As it was, my passage to Australia was booked. It looked the devil. Indeed, had it not been for the rescuing generosity of my American publishers I should have spent two of the most uncomfortable months of my existence. Even as it was, I arrived in Tahiti with a capital consisting of the unexpired portion of a ticket to Marseilles and eleven pounds in cash. I could see no alternative to continuing my journey. English short stories are an uncommercial commodity in a French island that has no printing press. The beachcomber market has been spoilt. And though I sent a cable of enquiry to the friend who manages my business, I had no reason for believing that anything but a substantial overdraft was awaiting me in London. Nor was anything unlikelier than that I should get an answer to my telegram in time.

Just occasionally, however, things turn out in real life as they do in stories. Hilaire Belloc has written somewhere of that dream of all of us, "the return of lost loves and great wads of unexpected wealth." And I do not think that any single moment will ever bring me, as it had never brought me, so keen a thrill as that with which I read on a green telegraph form, a few hours before the sailing of the ship, above the signature *Peters*, the news that one of the big American magazines had bought, and princelily, the serial rights of my last novel. I could not believe that it had really happened; that for half a year I was to be free from all need to worry about money; that I could stay in Tahiti as long as I might choose, that I could do the conventionally romantic thing and watch from the quay my ship sail on without me.

That evening I walked slowly and alone along the water-front. The air was heavy with the scent of jasmine. A car drove by; a rackety old Ford packed full on every seat, so that the half-dozen or so men and women in it were sitting anyhow on each other's laps, their arms flung about each other's shoulders. In their hair was the starred white of the *tiare*. One of them was strumming on a banjo; their voices were raised, their rich soft voices, in a Hawaiian tune. Here, indeed, seemed the Eden of heart's longing. Here was happiness as I had never seen it and friendliness as I had never seen it. Here was a fellowship that was uncalculating and love that was unpossessive, that was a giving, not a bargaining. I wondered how I should ever find the heart to leave.

Which is how most of us feel on our first evening in Tahiti, and yet, one by one, we wave farewell to the green island in the sure knowledge that in all human probability we have said good-bye to it for ever.

§

The conditions of the old South Sea sagas have been reversed. They told, those old stories, of men happening by chance on Eden, and suddenly abandoning their plans, and their ambitions, deciding that "slumber is more meet than toil," and letting their ship sail without them.

> To come as most men deemed to little good,
> But came to Oxford and their friends no more.

And that is over. You cannot at this late day happen unexpectedly upon a South Sea Island. The hydrographers have seen to that. Instead, the islands attract from a distance of ten thousand miles those whom modern life has disenchanted. It is with the half-confessed intention of never coming back that they set out. After they have been there ten days they assure you that no power on earth will induce them to go away, and yet within a very few weeks you will run across them in a shipping office.

Not, I think, for any of the obvious reasons.

I know all that can be urged against the tripperishness of Tahiti. It has a tourist agency, a cinema, six hotels and three ice-cream parlours, with the night-club idea of a good time so thoroughly introduced that all that the average Tahitian wants is to wear a print dress copied from a Californian fashion plate, be stood cocktails all the afternoon, taken to a cinema in the evening, and driven afterwards along the beach in a closed Buick. The whole island lives for the monthly arrival of the mail boat from San Francisco. During the twenty hours that the liner is moored against the quay every truck and car that comes in from the districts is packed. From dawn to closing time the tables of the Mariposa Café are crowded. There is not a seat vacant in the cinema, and afterwards there is dancing and singing and much drinking, so that the superior-minded tourist will raise his eyebrows scornfully. "I don't want to see this," he says. "I want to see the real island life."

But in point of fact the thing that he is seeing is the real island life. Except in remote islands the old Polynesian life has disappeared, and it is reluctantly against their will that those few still lead it. They would all prefer to be living in an imitation of the world that they have seen portrayed for them on the films. For that is the paradox of the islands: that we should go there a little wearied, a little disenchanted by the conditions of modern life to find a people whose one ambition is to establish in their green fastnesses the precise conditions that we are fleeing from.

While I was staying in Moorea there was a native girl who used to paddle across the lagoon most mornings in her canoe. She did a certain amount of work about the place, but most of her time she spent with a ukulele across her knees, humming Polynesian tunes, telling us Polynesian legends. It is of her that I think when I try to picture Loti's Rarahu. She was simple and friendly and affectionate. In the accepted sense she was not beautiful. She would have looked ugly in a photograph or in European dress. But when she danced, or sang, or swam she achieved a perfect harmony with that setting of palm trees and golden sand. She belonged there. And it was exquisite to watch her swimming under the water; the brown arms and shoulders, the scarlet and yellow pareo, the long black hair floating behind her like a comet's fan.

Here was the eternal Rarahu. And this, I told myself, was the Polynesia that existed before traders and missionaries came to tamper with it. This was what made Captain Cook's mariners desert their ship and hide in the green valleys.

As it was, of course. But it was a life that no longer contented the Polynesian. She was bored, insufferably bored. Her relatives kept her like a slave, she told me. They would not let her go to Tahiti. All her cousins were there enjoying themselves, going to cinemas, driving in Ford cars; and here she was, wasting her best years in an island where there was no cinema and not a single car. What was there for her to do? It was a shame, wasn't it? And it would have been useless for me to tell her how worthless a thing was that town-life in comparison with her own. She had seen the American magazines, and on her rare visits to Papeete had been taken to the cinema. She had absorbed the night-club idea of what is a good time.

It is hard for the European and the American to escape a wistful longing for the Polynesia that is rapidly disappearing. If only, we think, we could put back the clock two hundred years; if only we had sailed the Pacific in the *Bounty* instead of the *Makura*.

The last week of my first visit to Tahiti I spent forty miles from Papeete, at a hotel run by an Hawaiian, that was more a family boarding-house than a hotel. There was not a white man within five miles of us. We ate at a long table, some dozen of us, for though there were not more than four bedrooms, it was a patriarchal establishment, and stray cousins would arrive with banjos and ukuleles to stay for a day, for five days, for a month; to sing and fish, and at night stretch themselves on the verandah. You never knew whom you would find next morning at the breakfast table. It was a Tahitian house. We lived on Tahitian food: on *poi*, that is, the baby octopus; on raw fish soaked in coconut; on little crabs that have to be eaten with one's fingers if one is to get the flavour of the sauce; on shrimps served in a sweet curry, a preparation of coconut and ginger; on *feis* and yam and bread-fruit baked in a native oven. By day we would bathe and fish. By night we would sing and dance on the verandah.

One morning we went, some eight of us, for a picnic into the interior, to a pool five or six miles up the valley, where in the old days the queen would bathe with her handmaidens. It was a circular pool some fifteen yards across, and the stream that fed it had worn the rock quite smooth so that you could slide for thirty feet down a sharp decline into the water. It was a couple of hours' trudge. As we drew near the pool the girls let down their hair, twining fern wreaths for it; the moment we arrived they pulled off their European petticoats and frocks, wrapped their red and white pareos beneath their arms, and scampered up the path to see who would be the first into the pool, while the boys without bothering to take off their clothes plunged in as they were, in their shirts and trousers, laughing and shouting to one another. It was a race to see how often one could get out of the pool, clamber up the hilly path to the top and slide down again.

Then some one suggested that it was time for food, and while the girls prepared a fire, the boys went up the valley in search of *feis* and bread-fruit. By the time they were back the fire had been lit. They tossed the fruit among the red-hot ashes, and cutting a bamboo shoot they filled one end with the shrimps, the other with the small fish that they had chased and caught with their five-pronged spears on the way up the valley. They squeezed the juice of a lime over the fish, placed the bamboo in the centre of the fire, covered the fire with leaves and earth and twigs and went back to bathe and shout and laugh till the meal was ready.

It was a delightful meal; the best picnic food that I have ever eaten, and as I sat there on the rocks among those light-hearted, care-free people, the girls in their wreaths and pareos, the boys with their clothes still dripping from their bathe, it was with an intolerable sense of loss that I remembered that in five days I should be saying good-bye to all of this, perhaps for ever; saying good-bye not only to these cool valleys and this happy people, but to rarer things I could not afford to lose: to candour, innocence, simplicity. Where else could they be found? And how much longer would it be possible to find them here? In a few years' time civilisation would have made an end of the island life. A few years and Papeete would be rivalling Waikiki. What Papeete was now, Tautira would become. There would be houses and neat gardens and proficiency. A calculating people bent on "getting on in life."

It may be that it is as profitless and sentimental to lament the passing of Tahiti as it is to lament in Europe the passing of the peasant and the migration to the towns. The truest excellence is in simplicity. But between the simplicity of the peasant and the simplicity of men such as Turgenev is set the gradual evolution of centuries of thought. It may be that the simplicity of the peasant has to be destroyed, that life has to become complicated and obscure before the ultimate simplicity can be reached; that the only significant simplicity is based upon sophistication, upon experience and growth; that the passing of Tahiti is inevitable, that it is idle to regret it. It may be so. I think it is so. But I know that to the end of my life I shall be unable to recall without regret those tranquil moments in that valley; the green and yellow of the trees, the grey pool in front of us, the sound of water, and the girls with fern wreaths in their hair.

§

It is only at moments now that one catches glimpses of the old Polynesian life, and it may well seem that a visit to the South Seas must be as disenchanting an experience as life can offer. One does not travel ten thousand miles for the sake of finding the "Green Grotto" in a different setting.

But it is not quite like that; it is not that at all. For though the islanders may have a night-club idea of a good time, they do see to it that the time is good. They have none of that attitude of modish boredom that most townsfolk assume in restaurants and theatres. The Tahitians, into everything they do, throw a refreshingly primitive gusto for enjoyment. They would never go to a cinema because they had an odd half-hour to put in, because they had nothing better to do, because there are worse places to talk quietly and hold hands. They go there to see the pictures and to enjoy the pictures, and if volume of sound is any criterion of enjoyment they succeed. A bull-fight is the only public entertainment of which I can conceive as being noisier.

The noise starts at three o'clock in the afternoon when, shortly after the close of the siesta, a small cart covered with placards is driven round Papeete to an ear-splitting accompaniment of kettledrums. That is only a prelude. The noise inside the hall is deafening. To start with, the small urchins who occupy the front rows do not cease shrieking with laughter and excitement for one instant. There is a native orchestra, which is accompanied vocally by a considerable section of the audience. And, lastly, there is an interpreter to translate the cinema captions into Tahitian, whose voice has to make itself heard above the uproar. The cumulative effect would shame a football crowd at Stamford Bridge. How much the actual film conveys to the audience I cannot judge. Not a great deal, I fancy, at any rate in the way of continuous narrative. They do not see the various incidents as consecutive to one another. In the Paumotas Archipelago, for instance, where they can get hold of nothing except old and tattered serials, no attempt is made to arrange the instalments in any order. The fifteenth follows the third, and the first is sandwiched between the eleventh and the sixteenth, an arrangement that in no way lessens the hilarious delight of the native, who asks to be presented with a succession of sensations—a chase, a fight, a kiss— and does not care in what order the sensations follow.

The Tahitians have more sophisticated tastes, but the

part of the evening that they enjoy most is, I suspect, the twenty minutes' break in the middle of the long film, when the most succulent episodes out of the next week's programme—the fight, the chase, the kiss—are rushed through without explanation or caption, presumably as an advertisement, but actually as the chief attraction of the evening. The serious student of the cinema would not derive much entertainment from such an evening, but it is an experience that the spectator of the human comedy would be sorry to be without.

As is the case with the majority of those incidents that make up the sum of island life: the market, for instance, where the natives congregate every morning to buy their provisions and exchange the gossip of the previous night. And the daily departure of the district bus; you would search Europe in vain for its equivalent. It is an uncomfortable three hours' journey over an uneven road in a vast van lined with wooden seats; but there are many who prefer it, not only for reasons of economy, to a well-sprung Buick. It is an hilarious business. Invariably the truck is packed beyond capacity with baskets of fruit and vegetables and sacks of copra and such live stock as hens and pigs, among which the passengers arrange themselves as best they may. And they are all friends together and they shout the local scandal and the local jokes to one another. And every few minutes there is some one to get on and some one to get off, and the gossip of fresh districts to be exchanged. And there is a gaiety and gusto in that journey for which you will look in vain elsewhere.

Little remains of the life that Captain Cook discovered. But then you can find nowhere an exact replica of conditions that existed two hundred years ago. And possibly, since we ourselves are different, we should not appreciate them if we could. Possibly all that we are wise to look for are equivalents of that which charmed our ancestors, and the Society Islands seem, from what I have seen and heard, to be the one place in the Pacific where an equivalent for the Melville atmosphere exists.

§

The wilder islands of the Melanesian groups are not possible. They are harassed with mosquitoes and malaria; the natives are cowardly, savage and uninteresting. Samoa is under British control, which means the drawing of a sharp colour line, and though the drawing of that line is admirable and necessary in India and Malaya it is in search of freedom that you go to the South Sea Islands. Hawaii is too near America—only five days from San Francisco—with not only colour prejudices, but prohibition. Honolulu is nothing but a very charming American city, a holiday resort for Californians, an alternative to Del Monte. While the smaller Polynesian islands, which are little more than trading stations, are neither one thing nor another. Nothing that I have heard about the Marquesas has made me anxious to visit them.

Tahiti and Moorea alone provide an equivalent for what the mariners of the *Bounty* found, and that on the surface they very adequately do. In the first place they are French, and since the French are without colour prejudice you can, without social ostracism, mix freely with one of the gentlest and sweetest natured peoples in the world. They are in the very centre of the Pacific, a fortnight from Sydney, ten days from San Francisco. The mail boats visit them only once a month. There is, in consequence, no casual tourist traffic. You have to stay there a month or not at all. During the month's interval between the boats you are cut off completely from civilisation. There is no local newspaper, and no one bothers to read the wireless bulletin that is posted daily on the notice board outside the post office. You have, however, many of the amenities of civilisation. There are a number of hotels. And though they would seem in a photograph desolate and barren shacks, all you need in the tropics is a verandah, a shower-bath, and a comfortable bed.

The climate, apart from the two or three months of the rainy season, is delightful. Except at midday, it is never really hot. A thin Panama hat is sufficient protection against the sun. There is no malaria, the mosquitoes are small and not really troublesome. All night there is a sufficient breeze from the mountains to warrant at least one blanket on the bed, so that you get, what you so rarely get in the tropics, a night's rest that genuinely refreshes you. Living is very cheap, though not as cheap as it is supposed to be. The beachcomber market has been spoilt. Third-class passengers have to deposit their return fares before they are allowed to land. And those white men who have arrived practically penniless in the belief that they will be supported by native hospitality have been bitterly disappointed. Even so, living is cheap. There is little to spend money on. If you are going to settle there it is as well to arrive with enough money to build or buy a house, but a house once built, a married couple can live in very reasonable comfort on four hundred pounds a year, while with a thousand they can lead a life that six thousand would not give them in California.

Moreover, the life itself there is extremely pleasant. Though you are cut off from civilisation, you have no lack of varied and entertaining society. There are always a number of amusing people staying and passing through, and in a world where there is no strain nor hurry you have the leisure and amplitude for talk, for the free development of personal contacts. The days pass pleasantly.

"But what do you find to do there?" people ask. And that is a question which it is very hard to answer. One never seems to be doing anything in particular, and yet one is never bored. The air is warm and soft, and you relax to it as you relax to a hot bath. Though that is scarcely an exact simile. For you do not feel languid, but in abundantly good health. It is just that you can be happy taking a long time over everything; over dressing, over feeding pigeons, over wandering along the shore, collecting shells, sitting on a rock watching the many-coloured fish swim in and out among the coral, watching the land-crabs scurry away into their holes as you go by, sitting on a verandah listening to a Tahitian strum upon a ukulele. While all about you is the unbelievable beauty of the island; its flowered greenery and the marvel of its nights, its moonless as its moonlit nights; for when there is no moon the natives go out in their canoes to fish by torchlight, and from the verandah of your bungalow you watch the lights moving and swaying on the reef.

The days pass, you work a little and you play a little.

36

Life is effortless and sweet. And you wonder how you will ever find the heart to leave, and you ask yourself why you ever should. Here the best of both worlds seem to be combined. Surely here one should be able to forget all that is petty and contentious in western life, relaxing to this tranquil atmosphere, taking root here by these gentle waters.

§

And yet one cannot. One by one we have found, those of us who have made the experiment, that there is something in the atmosphere of Tahiti that prevents the modern sophisticated westerner from that relaxing. He cannot forget Europe. He cannot take root. And before he has been there many weeks he is beset by the last thing that he had expected to be beset by there, a curious restlessness and irritability. His nerves are on edge. He cannot settle down to anything. He loses all sense of proportion. He embarks on the most absurd quarrels with his acquaintances. He loses the very thing he came in search of, tranquillity.

Looking back in a calm remembrance of all that happened there, I have wondered sometimes whether it is not to the monthly arrival of the mail boat as much as anything that this restlessness is due. It introduces the idea of time, whereas timelessness is the essential condition of island life. A few days before my first visit there I dropped and broke my watch. It did not matter much on board a ship, and in Papeete I would get myself another one, I thought. But when I reached Tahiti I found that I had no need of a watch. Hours did not matter.

When the sun rose you got up. When the sun was high you siestaed. When the sun sank you began to think of supper.

During my six weeks there I had no watch and never missed it. And it seemed to me a fitting symbol of a return to western life that practically my first act on my return to San Francisco should be to buy one. I was back in a world where time mattered. And it is one of those curious coincidences that make one credulous of unseen presences that on my journey back, five months later, the dollar watch that I had bought in San Francisco, that had shepherded me without failing through America, through three months of London and across the Atlantic, through the West Indies and Panama into the Pacific, should, within a day's sail of Fakarava, have unaccountably and permanently stopped, as though it had realised that its work was finished and that I should have no further need of it in a country where time did not exist.

Or rather where time should not exist. For time does exist there now. The year is divided into the thirteen arrivals of the mail boats, and it is hard to imagine a more irritating spacing out of time. If the mail boat came every day it would be a matter of such ordinary occurrence that no one would notice it. If it came once a year you could forget about it in the interval. But once every four weeks; no, that is too much. By the time you have ceased talking about one mail you are talking about the next. The island life is built round mail day. It is the great gala day, for which the girls prepare their brightest frocks and the hotel proprietors their dearest wine. Instinctively, you find yourself counting the days to it, counting days in a country where you should lose count of days; counting the days to that which represents everything that you are trying to forget: letters, newspapers, the rivalries, jealousies and animosities to which you are still half attached; with people who are a part still of that life exchanging ideas with you, recalling to you ambitions you had thought were dead. The three days when a boat is moored against the wharf constitute a complete uprooting of the detachment you had been cultivating. They prevent you from taking root, and it is impossible to be at peace in a place where you cannot take root.

For a month, for two months, for three months possibly, you will imagine yourself to be in Eden, but sooner or later that restlessness, that irritability, will come. Your nerves will get on edge, and suddenly you will find yourself thinking that if you have to stay there another week you will go off your head. It is an experience that is almost universal. Nearly every one I know has sworn, a week before they left, that there was no spot in the world they hated more. And yet when the last syren goes, one and all we feel that our hearts are breaking. The first time I saw a ship sail from Papeete, a French naval officer, who was returning home by it, burst into tears. It was ridiculous, he said "mais on s'attache."

That is how most of us feel when we watch the mountains of Moorea grow indistinct.

§

It may be, though, that that explanation is too fanciful: that I came nearer to the truth in the story that I planned

39

and never wrote, of a young man who had decided to spend nine months in travel before taking up the partnership that his father's death had left open for him in the motor business, on whose proceeds he had been expensively educated at Marlborough and Magdalen. He would be the average romantically unexceptional young man, and like so many others when he saw the peaks of the Diadem he would order his steward to pack his trunks. "New Zealand and Samoa can wait," he had thought. "I've four months to spend. I'll spend them here."

I had pictured him that evening leaning over the balcony of the Hotel Minerva watching the sun set behind Moorea. Beside him there would be Demster, an English tourist, of a month's standing, whom all that afternoon the young man would have been cross-examining with an eager curiosity. Which is how usually it happens. For one arrives a stranger without introductions, and it is from a fellow tourist that one receives one's first and invariably inaccurate information on the island's customs.

"I wonder what you'll make of it," the older man was saying. "I suppose it'll end in your taking a house in the country somewhere and that'll mean an island marriage. It's the only way, I'm told, of getting a girl to cook for you. No one bothers about money here. And a girl would consider herself insulted if a bachelor asked her to work for him without living with him. They're simple folk. Frocks and motor rides and love. That's their whole life. I don't suppose that if you took a house you'ld be allowed to remain long in it alone."

But the young man, Ray Girling, would be scarcely listening. Curiosity would be at rest. The velvet of the night would be soft with the scent of jasmine, and down the lamp-lit avenue under the tent of the flamboyants, arm in arm the flower-haired girls are walking. The air is fragrant with a sense of love, sensual and tender love, such as the acuter and bitter passions of the north are alien to.

"I expect," he said, "I shall leave life to decide that for me."

It would be the typical opening to the conventional South Sea story, and indeed it is difficult to write otherwise than conventionally of Polynesia. It is as hard not to echo Loti as it is for the writer of detective stories to avoid parallels with Sherlock Holmes. But Rarahu is fifty years away; the death of Lovaina during the influenza epidemic marked the close of a *régime* as definitely as did for England the death of Queen Victoria. The issue is not the same now as it was for Maugham and Loti. And it was not merely the need for variety that made me plan the story about a white girl rather than a brown.

For that evening as the two men were walking along the water-front a voice hailed them, and two young women who had been riding towards them jumped off their bicycles.

"What, still here and still alone, and on a Tahitian evening?"

It was the elder who spoke, an American, gay-eyed and mischievous, married for ten years to a French official; much wooed by the younger Frenchmen and by none of them, rumour had it, with success, she was held to be the most attractive woman in Papeete. But it was the younger that Ray Girling noticed. Never had he seen any one to whom the trite simile of flower-like could be more appro-

41

priate. She was small and slight, with pale yellowish hair and cornflower-blue eyes. Her body in its pale green sheath of muslin seemed in truth to sway like a stem beneath the weight of the blossom that was her face.

Introductions followed.

"I don't think," said Demster, "that either of you know Mr. Girling. He arrived this morning on the *Makura*, and he fell in love with Tahiti so much that he's decided to stay on."

The American raised her eyebrows meaningly.

"In love, why, sure, but with an island!"

They laughed together.

"I can't think," said Girling, "how I shall find the heart to leave."

"That's what you all say at the beginning," said the girl whom he had noticed first.

"And do they all go away?"

She shrugged her shoulders.

"Some stay, of course; most go. To most people Papeete is a port of call. There're the tourists who stop for a month or two, and the officials who've come for three or four years, sometimes for half a lifetime. And the naval officers who are stationed on and off for a couple of years. Then there're a few Americans who spend their summers here. But in the end they go, nearly all of them. If you live here, you have rather a sad feeling of being— oh, how shall I put it?—like a station through which trains are passing. People come into your life and go out of it. It's like living in a hotel rather than in a home."

"But you're happy here?"

She pouted.

"It grows monotonous, you know."

"To me it seems like the Garden of Eden."

Again the cornflower-blue eyes smiled softly.

"I wonder if you'll be saying that in four months' time. You know what they say about Tahiti? That a year's too little a time to stay here and a month too long. They may be right. But when I was a child I always used to wonder whether Adam and Eve were really sorry to be cast out of Eden. I always wondered what they found to do there; didn't you, sometimes?"

She spoke half whimsically, half wistfully, in a voice that was lightly cadenced and with that particular purity of accent that is to be found only in those to whom English has come as a "taught language," a purity that seemed in its peculiar way symbolic of her charm.

"Perhaps," Ray Girling answered her. "But I'm very sure that I shall be heartbroken when the time comes for me to go."

At that point the American interrupted him.

"Heartbroken," she cried, "it won't be so much Mr. Girling who'll be heartbroken."

Again there was a general laugh.

"At any rate," she concluded, "I hope you won't get too domesticated to come and see us sometimes."

The invitation was made friendlily and genuinely enough, but it was of her companion that he was thinking as he accepted it, and it was about Colette that he sought information of Demster the moment they were alone.

"Who is that girl?" he asked. "You haven't met her before, I gather?"

Demster shook his head.

"I know all about her, though. It's rather a sad story. Her father was a Canadian who came over here to direct a store; her mother was a young French girl who fell in love with him and married him. Four years later, when the time came for the man to return to Montreal, he calmly informed her that he had a wife in America; that if she wished to have him arrested as a bigamist she could; but that if she did, his income and means of supporting her would cease; that the best thing would be for her to say nothing and to accept the allowance he would continue to send her, provided she made no attempt to leave the island: For Colette's sake she decided to accept. But every one knows, of course, as every one knows everything in Papeete. It's a sad story."

Girling nodded. He could understand now the wistful expression of those pale cornflower-blue eyes; he could understand why she had spoken wistfully of the station through which trains hurried, and he could imagine with what weight even in this free-est of free countries the knowledge of her parentage must press on her. "She must always feel," he thought, "apart from others. Never able to mix wholeheartedly among them." Yet in spite of it all her nature had not soured. "I hope," he thought, "that that isn't the last I'm going to see of her."

That was how the story was to have begun. The next scene was to have been at the cinema, three weeks later.

§

Four times a week there is a cinema performance in Papeete, and on those evenings the streets and cafés of the town are empty. And as Ray Girling stood on the steps of the long tin building during the ten minutes' interval, it was to seem to him that there were clustered in the street below, round the naphtha-lighted stalls where the little Chinese proprietors were making busy trade with ices and coconuts and water melons, every single person with whom he had been brought in contact during his stay in the hotel.

There was Tania, one of the last direct descendants of the old royal family of the Pomaris, her black hair dressed high upon her head, a rose silk Spanish shawl about her shoulders, chattering to the half dozen or so girls with whom he would idle most afternoons away over ice creams in the Mariposa Café. There was the Australian trader with whom he would discuss the relative merits of Woodfull and Macartney. A couple of French officials he had met at the *Cercle Coloniale* and others whom he knew by sight, the girls from the post office, the assistants from the three big stores, the skipper of the *Saint Antoine;* all that numerous crowd that he had watched from the balcony of his hotel, strolling lazily along the harbour-side. He had learnt to recognise most of the people in the town by sight during that three weeks' stay.

And he had done most of the things that one does do at Tahiti during one's first three weeks there. He had driven out round the island, through Mataiea, past the short wooden pier on which during the last spring of the world's peace a doomed poet wrote lines for Mamua. He had spanned the narrow isthmus of Taravao; he had lunched at Keane's off a sweet shrimp curry; he had bathed on the dark sands at Arue, and in the cool waters of the Papeno

River. He had chartered a glass-bottomed boat and, sailing out towards the reef, had watched the fish swimming in and out of the many-coloured coral. And day after day the sun had shone out of a blue sky ceaselessly and night after night moonshine and starlight had brooded over the scented darkness, and Ray Girling was beginning to feel just ever such a little bored.

"It may be," he thought, "that that girl was right about a year being too little a time and a month too long."

And gazing a little despondently at the thronged roadway, he wondered how he should employ the fourteen or so weeks that must pass before the sailing of the *Louqsor*, the French cargo boat, by which he had planned to return to Europe.

"Well," a voice was asking at his elbow, "and is it still the Eden that you expected?"

The question was so appropriate to his mood that he could not resist laughing as he turned to meet the smiling flowerlike features of Colette Garonne.

"At that precise moment," he said, "I was just wondering whether you weren't right about Adam and Eve finding it a little dull in Eden."

"You too, then, and so soon."

"I was just feeling . . ." But she was so divinely pretty, even under the harsh glare of the electric lights, that he could not retain his temper of despondency. "I was just feeling," he said instead, "what an enormous pity it was that we couldn't go on to supper and a cabaret after this, as we would if we were in New York or London."

"So you've come all this way to regret New York."

46

TAHITI

"To regret that there's nothing to do after eleven; for there isn't, is there?"

"Not in the way of cabarets."

"In any way, then?"

She pouted.

"The Bright Spirits drive off now and again in cars."

"In cars, where?"

"Oh, anywhere. To bathe, or out to Keane's, or just to sing. That's the island idea of cabaret."

"Well, then . . ." He hesitated. Often as he had sat before going to bed on the hotel verandah he had envied the crowded cars that had driven singing through the night below him. It had seemed so care-free and light-hearted with a light-heartedness with which he was not in tune. But he had felt always shy of suggesting such an expedition to any of his friends. On this occasion, however, the impelling influence of pale blue eyes emboldened him. "Wouldn't it be rather fun," he said, "to have an impromptu cabaret this evening?"

It was her turn to hesitate. "Well," she said, pausing doubtfully.

He could tell what was passing in her mind. Though he had seen her often enough, smiling greetings at her, they had not talked together since the night when Demster had introduced them. And she was uncertain, he could guess that, as to the types of companion that he would be selecting for her. He made no effort, however, to persuade her. He had the intuition to realise that at such moments it is the wiser plan not to urge the reluctant to say "Yes," but to make it difficult for them to say "No."

47

Less than a yard away Tania was chattering noisily in the centre of a crowd of friends, and stretching out his hand, Ray Girling touched her on the arm.

"Tania," he said, "we were thinking of driving out somewhere after the show. What's your idea of it?"

"Sweetheart, that it would be heavenly."

"And who else'll come?"

Tania glanced round her slowly.

"There's you, and I, and Colette, and Marie; and we'd better have Paul to amuse Tepia."

In a minute or two it had been arranged.

"Then we'll meet," said Girling, "outside Gustave's the moment the show's over."

§

It was one of those nights that are not to be found elsewhere than in Tahiti. It was October and the night was calm. From the mountains a breeze was blowing, swaying gently the white-flowered shrubs along the road, ruffling ever so slightly the languidly bending palms. Westwards over the Pacific, a long street of silver to the jagged outline of Moorea, was a waxing moon; clouds moved lazily between the stars. The air was mild, sweet scented with the tiare, a sweetness that lay soft upon their cheeks as the car swayed and shook and rattled eastwards. The hood of the car was up, for in Tahiti there is always a possibility of rain: and for the islanders the landscape is too familiar to be attractive in itself. It is for the sensation of speed that motoring is so highly valued an entertainment. And as the car swayed over the uneven road,

48

they laughed and sang, beating their hands in time with the accordion.

For an hour and a half they drove on, singing under the stars.

"Where are we going?" asked Ray at length. "Isn't it time we were thinking about a bathe?"

"Not yet, sweetheart," laughed Tania. "Let's see if Keane's up still."

"At this hour?"

"One never knows."

For there are no such things as regular hours in the Islands. One is up certainly with the sun, and usually by nine o'clock in the evening one is thinking about bed; but there is always a possibility that friends will come: that a car will stop outside your bungalow: that a voice will cry, "What about driving to Papeno?" And you will forget that you were sleepy, and a rum punch will be prepared, and there will be a banjo and an accordion, and there will be singing and Hula-Hulas, and hours later you will remember that a car is in the road outside, that you were planning to bathe in the Papeno River, and, laughing and chattering, you will stumble out of the bungalow, pack yourselves anyhow into a pre-war Ford and, still laughing and still singing, you will drive away into the night, to wrap pareos around you and splash till you are a-weary in the cool, fresh mountain stream. It is an island saying that no night has ended till the dawn has broken, and at Keane's there is always a chance of finding merriment long after the streets are silent in Papeete. And sure enough, "Look, what did I say?" Tania was crying a few moments later. Through the thick tangle of trees a light was glimmering; there was the sound of a gramophone and clapping hands.

There were some dozen people on the verandah when they arrived; a planter from Taravao had stopped on his way back from Papeete for a rum punch; there had been a new record to try on the gramophone, some boys on their way back from fishing had seen lights and had heard singing, one of Keane's daughters had taken down her banjo and a granddaughter of Keane's had danced Hula-Hulas, while beakers of rum punch had been filled and emptied; twenty minutes had become five hours and no one had thought of bed. It was after midnight, though, and probably, without the arrival of any fresh incentive, in another half hour or so the party would have broken up. As it was, a cry of eager welcome was sent up as Girling's car drove up, and another half dozen glasses were bustled out, another beaker of rum punch brewed, and Tania, seated cross-legged upon the floor, her banjo across her knees, was singing that softest and sweetest of Polynesian songs,

> Ave, Ave, te vahini upipi
> E patia tona, e pareo repo,

that haunting air that will linger for ever in the ears of those that hear it; that across the miles and across the years will wake an irresistible nostalgia for the long star-drenched nights of Polynesia, for the soft breezes, and the bending palm trees, the white bloom of the hibiscus, and the murmur of the Pacific rollers on the reef; for the sights and sounds and scents, for the flower-haired, dark-skinned people of Polynesia. And as Tania sang and the girls danced, and the men beat their hands in time, the magic and beauty of the night filled overbrimmingly, as thriftlessly poured wine a beaker, the Western mind and spirit of Ray Girling.

"There's nothing like it," he murmured. "Not in this world, certainly."

"Nor probably," quoted Colette, "in the next."

And he remembered how a few hours earlier, in a mood of boredom, he had thought of Tahiti as a frame without a picture. He could understand now why he had felt like that. He had been looking at it from the outside. One had to surrender to Tahiti, to let oneself be absorbed by it.

Something of this sentiment he tried to convey to Colette.

"It's no good," he said, "looking at Tahiti from outside."

She sighed. "Outside. But that's what so many of us have to be."

He looked down at her in surprise.

"Outside! You!"

"It's not always so easy to surrender. You've got to surrender so much else as well." She paused, looked up at him, questioningly, then seeing that his eyes were kind, continued: "For me to be absorbed in it, for me to be inside this life, it would mean living the same life as all these other girls, and, well, you know what that is. I just couldn't; it's not that I'm a prude, but you know what my life's been; my mother's had a bad time. I'm all she's got. It would break her if anything were to happen to me."

"If you were to marry, though."

She laughed, a little bitterly. "But who's to marry me? Who, at least, that I'ld care to marry. There aren't so many white men here. It's not for marriage that the tourist comes. The English and the Americans who settle here as often as not have left wives behind them. At any rate they've come because they've tired of civilisation. They're not the type that makes a conventional marriage. And though the French may be broadminded about liaisons, they're very particular about marriages. As far as they're concerned I'm damaged goods. It's not even as though I had any money. And I can't go. I can't leave my mother. I'm not complaining. Please don't think that. I'm pretty happy really. But I've never felt, I don't suppose I ever shall feel, as though I really belonged here."

She had spoken softly, her voice sinking to a whisper; and as Ray Girling listened, a deep feeling of pity overcame him. She was so sweet, so pretty; it was cruel that life should have been harsh to her, here of all places, in Tahiti. It was true, though, what she had said. What they had both said about belonging here. One had to surrender to Tahiti, to take it on its own terms. Otherwise for all time there would be an angel before that Eden, with the drawn sword that was the knowledge of good and evil. He had talked a few minutes since of being himself inside it, but that he could never be as long as he was content to remain a sojourner. He was just a tourist like any other, with his life and interests ten thousand miles away. He had a few weeks to spend here: a few weeks in which to gather as many impressions as he could. And perhaps because he loved the place so well, something of

its mystery would be laid on him. But it was not thus
and to such as he that Tahiti would lay bare her secrets.
You had to come empty-handed to that altar; you had to
surrender utterly; you could not be of Tahiti and of
Europe. You would have to cut away from that other
life, those other interests. Your whole life must be
bounded by Tahiti; you must take root there by the
palm-fringed lagoons, and then, little by little, you would
absorb that magic. The spirit of Tahiti would whisper
its secrets into your ear. You must surrender or remain
outside. Wistfully he looked out over the verandah.

It was so lovely, the garden with its tangled masses of
fruits and flowers. The dark sand, with the faint line of
white where the water rippled among the oyster beds; and
the long line of coast, swerving outwards to a hidden
headland, with beyond it, above the bending heads of the
coconut palms, the dark shadow that was the mountains
of Taravao; and over it all was the silver moonlight and
the music of the breakers on the reef; and here at his feet,
one with the magic of the night, were the dark-skinned,
laughing people to whose ears alone the spirit of Tahiti
whispered the syllables of its magic.

And as he leant back against the verandah railing there
came to him such thoughts as have come to all of us under
the moonlight on Tahitian nights. He thought of the
turmoil and the conflict that was Europe: the hurry and
the malice and the greed: the ceaseless battle for self-
protection: the ceaseless exploitation of advantage: the
long battle that wearies and hardens and embitters: that
brings you ultimately to see all men as your enemies, since
all men are in competition with you, since your suc-

cess can only be purchased at the price of another's failure. He thought of what his life would be for the next forty years; he contrasted it with the gentleness and sweetness and simplicity of this island life, where there is no hatred since there is no need for hatred; where there is no rivalry since life is easy, since the sun shines and the rain is soft, and the *feis* grow wild along the valleys, and livelihood lies ready to man's hand. Where there is no reason why you should not trust your neighbour, since in a world where there are no possessions there is nothing that he can rob you of; where you can believe in the softness of a glance, since in a world where there are no social ladders there is nothing that a woman can gain from love-making but love. Such thoughts as we all have on Tahitian nights. And thinking them, he told himself that were he to sell now his share in his father's business there would be a yearly income for him of some six hundred pounds, a sum that would purchase little enough in Europe, where everything had a market price, but that would mean for him in Tahiti a bungalow on the edge of a lagoon, wide and clear and open to the moonlight, and there would be so much of work as to keep idleness from fretting him; and there would be a companion in the bungalow, and children—smiling, happy children, who would grow to manhood in a country where there is no need to arm yourself from childhood for the fight for livelihood.

And at his elbow there was Colette, exquisite and frail and gentle. "Why run for shadows when the prize was here?" England seemed very distant, and very unsubstantial the rewards that England had for offering, and along the verandah railing his hand edged slowly to Colette's; his little finger closed over hers; her eyes through the half twilight smiled up at him. They said nothing; but that which is more than words, that of which words are the channels only, had passed between them. And on the next morning when Ray Girling, along with the half of Papeete, was strolling down the water-front to welcome the American courier, he blushed awkwardly when he heard himself hailed by the gay-toned American voice. "Hullo, hullo," she called. "And it's a whole month since we said good-bye to Mr. Demster, and you're still living virtuously at Gustave's!" He blushed, for Colette was at her side, and her eyes were smiling into his, and between them the thought was passing that the time was over for him to make an Island marriage.

"I've got three months left," he laughed. But it had ceased, he knew, to be a question of weeks and months. But of whether or not he was to make his home here in Tahiti. The magic of the Island and the softness of Colette had cast the mesh of their net about him: the net that in one way or another is cast on all of us who watch from the harbour-side our ship sail off without us. Of the many thousands who have loitered in these green ways there cannot be one who has not wondered, if only for an instant, whether he would not be wise to abandon the incessant struggle that lies eastward in America and Europe. Not one out of all those thousands.

§

Yet it is no longer true that those who come to the Islands rarely leave them. Sydney and San Francisco are very close. The story of most loiterers in Papeete is the story of their attempt not to commit themselves too far, to leave open a loophole for escape. Time passes slowly in the Islands, and usually before they have become too enmeshed something has happened to force on them the wisdom of delay.

For Girling it was the arrival by the *Manganui* of the liveliest thing in Australian salesmen that he had ever met. It happened shortly before ten o'clock. Like a whirlwind a short, plump, perspiring, serge-suited figure had hustled its way into the Mariposa Café, tossed its felt hat across a table, and leaning back in a chair had begun to fan its face with a vast brown silk handkerchief.

"My oath," it cried, "but this is the hottest place I've struck! My oath, but a gin sling would be right down bonza!"

The two waitresses who were leaning against the bar gazed blankly at him.

"My word, but you aren't going to tell me that you've got no ice!"

He spoke rapidly, with a marked Australian accent, and the girls who could only understand English when it was spoken extremely slowly, did not understand him. They looked at one another, then looked at the stranger, then looked again at one another and burst into laughter. It was time, Girling felt, that he came to the rescue of his compatriot.

"Suppose," he suggested, "that I were to interpret. These girls don't understand much beyond French."

"Now that would be really kind. And it would be kinder still if you were to order yourself whatever you like and join me with it. You will? Good-oh! That's bonza. You staying here? Well, I pity you. Myself? My oath, sir, no! When that boat sails for dear old Sydney I'll be on it. No place like Sydney in the world. Manly and Bondi and the beaches. Nothing like them. Dinky-die. New York can't touch it. Just come from there. Been travelling in wool. Did I sell much? My oath, sir, I did not. But I've learnt the way to sell. Those Yanks know how to advertise. Personal touch. Always gets you there. Straight at the consumer. Me addressing you, that's the way. The only way. Now look here," and lifting his eyes he began to glance round the room in search of some advertisement that would illustrate his point. " 'J'irai loin pour un camel,' " he slowly mispronounced; "don't know enough French to tell if that's good or not. Let's see. Ah, look now," and jumping to his feet he pointed excitedly to a large cardboard notice that had been hung above the bar.

"ASK GUSTAVE
HE KNOWS."

"That's it," he exclaimed. "Couldn't be better. No long sentences. Nothing about our being anxious to give any information that tourists may require. Nothing impersonal or official. Nothing to terrify any one. Just the impression of a friendly fellow who'll give you a friendly hand. The very impression you want to give. My oath it is!"

He began to enlarge his theme. He began to discuss American publicity; international trade and the different conditions in America and Australia; and Girling, as he sat there listening, found himself more interested than he

57

had ever been for months. He had been so long away from business. And when you got down to brass tacks was there a thing in the world half as thrilling? It was a game, the most exciting, and the highest prized. Your wits against the other man's. And as he sat there listening, Girling felt an itch to be back in that eager competitive society. He had always found that he did his best thinking when he was listening. Something said suggested a train of thought, and as the Australian's conversation rattled on an idea came suddenly to Girling for the launching of the new model his firm had been designing for the autumn. The exact note of publicity to get. He saw it; he knew it. Get a good artist to illustrate it, and for a few months anyhow they'ld have every one upon the market beat. His blood began to pound hotly through his veins.

And then, suddenly, he remembered: that there was going to be no return to London; there was going to be a selling of shares and the building of a bungalow: a succession of quiet days spent quietly; and an immense depression came on him, such a depression as one feels on waking from a pleasant dream: a depression that was followed by such a sensation of relief as one feels on waking from a nightmare. "It wasn't true. None of it had happened yet."

And while the Australian chattered on Ray Girling leant forward across the table, his head upon his hands. What did he want, to go or to stay? To go or stay? For he realised that he must make a choice, that it must be either England or Tahiti: that the one was precluded by the other. And was it really, he asked himself, that he was weary of the strife of London, that the secret of Polynesia was worth the surrender of all that until now he had held to make life worth living? Was it anything more than a mood, the bewitching effect of moonlight and still water and a pretty girl that was luring him to this Pacific Eden?

"I must think," he thought. "I mustn't decide hurriedly. Whatever happens, I must give myself time to think."

Even as he decided that he saw on the other side of the street beside the schooners, the trim, dainty figure of Colette. She was carrying a parasol: her head was bared, he saw all the daintiness of that shingled hair, and he caught his breath at the thought of saying "Good-bye" to so much charm and gentleness. "I'm not in love with her," he thought. "But in two days if I were to see more of her I should be. And if I were to fall in love with her, it would be in a way, I believe, that I'm never likely to be again. I shall be saying good-bye to a good deal if I catch the *Louqsor*."

That catching of his breath, however, had warned him that it must not be in Papeete that his decision must be come to. If he were to stay on at Gustave's, with the certainty of seeing Colette again in a day or two he knew only too well that he would commit himself irremediably.

"Whatever happens," he said, "I must get away for a week and think."

§

It is about forty miles from Papeete to Tautira, and every afternoon Gustave's truck, a vast van of a Buick,

59

lined with seats, makes the rocking three hours' journey there along the uneven island road. It is an uncomfortable, but by no means unpleasant journey. As the car jolted on past Paiea towards Papiieri a feeling of assuagement descended on the turmoil of Girling's spirit. He had been wise, he felt, to make this journey. Things were moving too fast for him in Papeete. He had need of the rest and quiet of the districts. He was carrying a letter of introduction to the chief, who would find room for him somewhere in his bungalow, and there would be long lazy mornings reading on the verandah, bathing in the lagoon, with tranquil evenings in the cool of the grass-grown pathways.

It was very warm inside the truck. Every seat was occupied, and since all the gossip had been exchanged and it was too hot for the effort of conversation, one of the drivers had taken out his accordion and was playing softly. Already they had left behind them the more formal districts; Papara and Paiea and Mataiea. They had passed the narrow isthmus of Taravao; the scenery was growing wilder. There had been little attempt made here to keep the gardens tended. Bungalows had been set down apparently at hazard, among the tangle of fruit and flowers; the women who were stretched out on mats on the verandahs no longer wore the European costume. It was over the white and red of the pareo that their black hair fell. In some such Tahiti as this it was that Loti loved. But it was vaguely that Girling was conscious of the landscape. His eyelids had grown heavy; tired by bright colours. His head began to nod.

He woke with a start and to the sound of laughter. "I

make nice pillow?" a voice was asking him. And blinking, he realised that his head had sunk sideways on to the shoulders of the girl who was beside him. She was tall and handsome, a typical Tahitian, with fine eyes and hair, and a laughing mouth.

"I'm so sorry," he began.

She only laughed, called out something in Tahitian to the driver, and taking Girling by the wrist, drew him back towards her.

"Bye-bye, baby," she said.

But Girling was now wide awake: vividly conscious of the girl beside him. Her coloured cotton dress was bare above the elbow, and through the thin silk of his coat he could feel the full, firm texture of her skin. She was strong and healthy with the glow and strength of native blood. Beneath her wide-brimmed, flower-wreathed straw hat she was laughing merrily, and as he leant a little more heavily against her arm she giggled and again called out in Tahitian to the driver. There was a ripple of laughter through the truck. Girling, flushing uncomfortably, drew away; but the girl smiled friendlily and drew him back.

"No, no," she said, "you tired, you sleep."

There was no sleep, though, now for him. But lest the excuse for nearness would be taken from him, he half closed his eyes and leant sideways against the soft, strong shoulder, conscious with a mingling half of excitement, half of fear that each minute was bringing them nearer to Tautira, that he and this girl would be close neighbours. It was not till they were within two hundred yards of the chief's house that she jerked her knee sideways against his.

"Wake up now," she cried. "My house here."

She stretched out her hand to him and as he took it, her fingers closing over his, pressed lightly for a moment. Her fine bright eyes were glowing, her full, wide mouth was parted in a smile. He hesitated, wondering whether to let the incident close. He decided to. They were in the same village, after all. They were bound to be seeing each other again. As the car rolled on along the road he leant out of the window to look back at her. She, too, had turned and, standing in the garden before her bungalow, waved her hand at him.

§

If all Tahiti is a garden then is Tautira Tahiti's garden. There still lingers something of the Polynesia that was before traders had corrupted and missionaries destroyed the faith of that gentle people. There is no white man living in Tautira. The roads are overgrown with grass. There are no fences and no boundary lines. Hens and pigs wander about the gardens and paths and houses as they choose. They will find their way home at evening. There is no one who could be troubled to steal. And since the meat market of Papeete is many miles away, the natives still live upon the produce of their hands: the fish they catch and spear and the bread-fruit that they bake.

The chief, a large, strong-hewn figure, clad only in a pareo, although he had not received a white visitor for several months, received Girling with no excitement or surprise, with a simple, unaffected welcome.

It would be quite easy, he said, to prepare a room for

him; and there would be some dinner ready in about an hour. He would not, he feared, be able to join him at it, for he had to supervise the evening's haul of fish. But they would have a long talk next day at lunch time. He had served in the French army during the War, winning the Médaille Militaire; they would doubtless have experiences to exchange. And with extreme courtesy he had left him.

It was cool and quiet in the house. But for all that the air was soft and the sunset a glow of lavender behind the palms, there was no peace for the spirit of Ray Girling. He was restless and ill-at-ease; his mind was busy with thoughts of the tall, bright-eyed girl, and after dinner, as he walked out along the beach, the memory of that firm, soft shoulder was very actual to him.

Should he be seeing her, he wondered; the chief had explained to him where the nets were being hauled ashore. As likely as not the greater part of the village would be assembled there. But probably she would have some other man with her. He had been a fool not to have spoken to her on the truck. Then had been his chance and he had let it slip. That is, if he had wished to be availed of it. And did he? He did not know. There were so many rival influences at work. He knew the speed of coconut wireless, how quick gossip was to spread. Days before he had left Tautira Colette would have heard of his adventure. He could not return to her after it. It would mean the end for ever of any thought of staying permanently on the island. For he knew that between himself and a girl such as the one he had sat next in the truck there could be no permanent relationship. There could be no question of love between them, on his side, anyhow. Very speedily he would have exhausted the slender resources of her interest. Nor, indeed, would she herself expect anything but a Tahitian Idyll. Tahitians were used to the coming and going upon ships. She would weep when he went away, but though there is tear-shedding there is no grief upon the Islands. She would console herself soon enough. If he were to yield to the enchantment of time and place he would have in the yielding answered that problem which had perplexed him. But did he want to? He did not know. Against the heady hour's magic was set the fear of loss: the loss of Colette, and also insidiously but painfully the loss of health. What did he know, after all, about this girl? And in that moment of indecision, in the forces that went to the framing of that indecision, he appreciated to the full in what manner and in what measure the coming of the white man had destroyed the simple beauty he had found. Even here one had to be cautious, to weigh the consequences of one's acts. And as he strolled beneath the palm trees to where he could see dark groups of clustered figures, he pictured that vanished beauty; pictured on such an island on such a night, some proud pirate schooner drawing towards the beach; pictured the dark-skinned people running down to welcome them, the innocence and friendliness of that hospitality; pictured the singing and the dancing, the large group breaking away gradually into couples, the slow linked strolling beneath the palms, the kissing and the laughter; the returning to the clean, fresh bungalows; the loving while loving pleased. And that was finished. Gone, irrecapturable, never to be found again upon this earth; never, never, never.

64

Still undecided, he walked on to take his place among the crowd gathered upon the beach.

It was a homely scene; the long row of men hauling at the nets, shouting and encouraging each other, and the women seated upon the sand, clapping their hands with pleasure as the fish were poured, a leaping, throbbing mass, into the large, flat-bottomed boats. Girling had not been standing there long before a hand had been laid upon his arm and a laughing voice was asking him: "Well, you not sleepy now?"

She had seemed attractive enough to him on the truck, but now hatless, with her dark hair flung wide about her shoulders, there was added a compelling softness to her power. And as he looked into her eyes, bright and shining through the dusk, her lips parted in a smile over the shining whiteness of her teeth, he felt that already the problem and his perplexity had been taken from him: that life had found his answer.

They sat side by side together on the bottom of an up-turned boat: very close so that her shoulder touched his: so that it seemed natural for him to pass his arm about her waist, for his fingers to stroke gently the firm, soft flesh of her upper arm. Afterwards, when the nets had been hauled in and the division of the fish arranged, they strolled arm in arm along the beach. From the centre of the village there came a sound of singing. In front of a Chinese store Gustave's truck had been arranged as a form of orchestral stand; the drivers had brought out their banjos, and on the wooden verandah of the store a number of young natives were dancing. They would sing and shout and clap their hands, then a couple would slither out into the centre and standing opposite each other would begin to dance. They would never dance more than a few steps, however. In less than a minute they had burst into a paroxysm of laughter, would cover their faces with their hands and run round to the back of the circling crowd.

"Come," said the girl, and taking Girling by the hand, she led him up into the truck. It was a low seat and they were in the shadow; the moment they were seated, without affectation, she turned her face to his, expressing in a kiss, as such sentiments were meant to be expressed, the peace and happiness of a Tahitian evening. And the moon rose high above the palm trees, lighting grotesquely the jagged peaks of the hills across the bay. The breeze from the lagoon blew quietly. Through the sound of the singing voices he could hear the undertone of the Pacific on the reef. Slowly, wooingly, the sights and scents and sounds that have for centuries in this fringe of Eden stripped the doubter of all thoughts of consequences, lulled Girling's doubts to rest. For a long while they sat there in the shadow of the car; her chin resting against his shoulder, his fingers caressing gently the soft surface of her cheek and arm.

"Tired?" she asked, at length.

He nodded. "A little."

"Then we go. You come with me?"

The question was put without any artifice or coquetry, as though it were only natural that thus should such an evening end.

His heart was thudding fiercely as they walked, quickly now, and in silence, down the path between low hedges towards her home. When they reached the verandah she lifted her finger to her lips. "Sh!" she said. "Wait."

There was a rustle, and a sound of whispers; the turning of a handle, the noise of something soft being pulled along the floor, then a whispered "Come," and a hand held out to him.

It was very dark. From the verandah beyond came the sound of movement. As he stepped into the room his toe caught on something, so that but for her hand he would have fallen. He stumbled forward on to the broad, deep mattress. For a moment he felt an acute revulsion of feeling. But two arms, cool and bare, had been flung about his neck, dark masses of hair scented faintly with coconut were beneath his cheek; against his mouth, soft and tender were her lips. His arm tightened about the firm, full shoulders, the tenderness of his kisses deepened, grew deep and fierce.

§

That people is happy which has no history. There are no details to a Tahitian Idyll.

There was a bungalow, half way towards Ventura. It was small enough, two rooms and a verandah, with little furniture; a table, a few chairs, a long, low mattress-bed. But there was a stream running just below it from the mountains; cool and sweet. Here at any hour of the day you could bathe at will. And there was green grass running down towards the sand; from the verandah you looked outwards towards Moorea, over the roof were twined and intertwined the purple of the bougainvillea, and the red and white and orange of the hibiscus, across the door was the gold and scarlet of the flamboyant, and when you have those things, you do not need furniture or pictures or large houses.

During the three months that he lived there Ray Girling went but rarely into Papeete, and during them he came as near as perhaps any sojourner can to understanding the spirit of Tahiti. It was a lazy life he led. When he was not bathing, he would lie out reading on the verandah; he ate little but what came from within a mile of his own house. Bread and butter came certainly from the town, but that was all. Once or twice a week he and Pepire would go up the valleys to collect enough lemons and bread-fruit and bananas to last for days. And her brother and cousin would always be coming from Papeete or Tautira, so that it was rare for Girling to wake in the morning without finding some visitors stretched out asleep on the verandah. They were profitable guests, however, for in the evening they would sail towards the reef and spear fish by torchlight or else they would go shrimping up the valleys, and afterwards, while Pepire would prepare the food, they would sit round with their banjos, singing.

And he was happy; happier than he had ever been. Had he not known that he was leaving in three months he would have probably looked forward with apprehension to the time when Pepire would have begun to weary him. As it was, he could accept without fear of consequences the day's good things. As Europe understands love he did not love her. He cared for her in the same way that he might have cared for some animal. And

68

indeed, as she strode bare-footed about the house and garden she reminded him in many ways of a cumbersome Newfoundland puppy. Her behaviour when she had transgressed authority was extraordinarily like that of a dog that has filched the cutlets. On one occasion she went into Papeete with a hundred-franc note to buy some twenty-five francs worth of stores. When Girling came in from his bathe, he found her standing with her hands behind her back, gazing shamefacedly at the pile of groceries on the table beside which she had laid a ten-franc note.

"Well, what's that?" he asked.

"The change," she told him.

"But how much did all that cost?"

"Twenty-seven francs."

"And ten makes thirty-seven, and fifteen for the truck, that's fifty-two. What's happened to the other forty-eight?"

She made no reply, but sheepishly and reluctantly she drew her hands from behind her back and produced the four metres of coloured prints with which she proposed to make a frock.

She was always surprising him in delightful ways. There was the occasion when he returned from Papeete with a rather pleasant Indian shawl. She surveyed it with rapture, but before she had thanked him she asked the price. And whenever any visitor came the first thing she would do would be to run and fetch the shawl and display it proudly with the words: "Look. He gave me. Five hundred francs!"

"I wonder," thought Girling, "whether the only difference between an English and a native girl is that what an

English girl thinks a Tahitian says, and what an English girl says a Tahitian does?"

It was only on occasions that he would wonder that. In the deeper things he realised how profound was the difference between brown and white. Had they been English lovers, loving under the shadow of separation, their love-making would have been greedy, fierce and passionate. But passion is a thing that the Islanders do not know. The Tahitians are not passionate. They are sensual and they are tender, but they are not passionate. Passion, though it may not be tragic, is at least potential tragedy, and tragedy is the twin child of sophistication. For Pepire, kisses were something simple and joyous and sincere. And yet during the long nights when she lay beside him Girling would wonder whether he would ever know in life anything sweeter than this love, so uncomplicated and direct. Intenser moments certainly awaited him, but sweeter . . . ? He did not know.

Once only during those weeks did he see Colette. A brief, pathetic little meeting. He had gone into the library at Papeete to change a book, and as he stood before the shelves, turning the pages of a novel, she came into the shop. It would have been impossible for them not to see each other.

"What ages since we met!" she said, and she, as well as he, was blushing.

"I don't come in often now," he said. "I'm living in the country."

"I know."

In those two syllables were conveyed all that his living in the districts meant.

"You're still going by the *Louqsor?*"

And in that question was implied that other question. How seriously was he taking his new establishment?

"Oh, yes, in another three weeks now."

"Then I'll see you then if not before."

With a bright smile she turned away. That, and no more than that.

And so the days went by.

Wistfully for him now and then.

For the closer that Ray Girling grew to the Tahitian life, the wider, he realised, was the chasm between him and it. He would never find the key to Tahiti's magic. And soon there would be no mystery left to find. A few years and Tahiti would be a second Honolulu. She was self-condemned. Somehow she had not had the strength to withstand the invader. And, looking back, it seemed to him symbolic that it should have been by the spirit of Tahiti that his determination to settle in Tahiti had been foiled. For it was the spirit of Tahiti expressed momentarily in Pepire that had entrapped him into the weakness that had made a permanent settlement there impossible. The fatal gift of beauty. It was by her own loveliness, her own sweetness, her own gentleness, that Tahiti had been betrayed. And yet it was back to the sweetness that it had destroyed, that ultimately the course of progress must return.

§

The monthly arrival of the American courier is the big event in the island life.

But, for all that, it is only on the departure of those rarer visitants, the *Louqsor* and the *Antinous*, that you get the spirit of an island leave-taking. For Tahiti is a French possession, and it is from the taffrail of the Messageries Maritimes boats that the French, who are the real Tahitians, who by long sojourning have identified themselves with the island life, wave their farewells to the nestling waterside.

For beauty and pathos there is little comparable with those last minutes of leave-taking. When the great liners sail from Sydney the passengers fling paper streamers to the waving crowds upon the wharf; but in Papeete there is no such attempt to prolong to the last instant the sundering tie. For those that were your friends upon the island have hung upon your neck the white wreath of the tiare and the stiff yellow petal of the pandanus, so that your nostrils may for all time retain the sweet perfume of Tahiti; and over your shoulders they have hung long strings of shells, so that you will retain for ever the soft murmur of the breakers on the reef, and it is not till you have forgotten those that you will forget Tahiti.

No ship has looked more like a garden than did the *Louqsor* in the January of 1927. There were many old friends to wave farewell from its crowded decks, some who were saying good-bye for ever, if any one can ever be said to say good-bye for ever, since for all time the memory of that green island will linger green. There were others who were going to France on leave for a few months. The Governor of the Island was returning to Paris for promotion. There were a number of officials; three or four naval officers; and on the lower decks a

74

large group of sailors from the *Casiope* returning to Marseilles. It was a gay sight. A squad of soldiers had lined
up to salute the Governor, a band was playing, the sailors
were singing farewell to their five days' sweethearts.

> Ave, Ave, te vahini upipi
> E patia tona, e pareo repo.

A few yards from Ray Girling, Colette, frail and dainty,
was smiling wistfully at him from beneath the shadow of
her parasol. As he saw her he turned away from the
crowd with whom he was gossiping—Pepire, Tania, and
the rest—and came across to her.

She received him with a smile.

"Do you remember saying four months ago that you'ld
be heartbroken when the time came for you to leave?"

"I remember."

"And are you?"

He hesitated, for as he looked down into the flowerlike face he knew the measure of his loss, knew what he
had missed, what there had been for finding; knew also
how impossible it would have been to find it, since certain
things precluded other things, since that which he had
been looking for bore no relation to the practical ordering
of life. When he answered, though it was in terms of
Tahiti that he spoke, it was of himself and her that he
was speaking.

"As long as I live I shall remember," he said, and his
voice was faltering. "And there'll be a great many times,
I know, when I shall regret bitterly that I ever came away.
But I shall know, too, that it would have been madness for
me to have stayed. I came at the wrong time. If I'd come

as a boy of twenty, before I'd begun European life, I could have stayed. Or I might have stayed if I'd come as a middle-aged man, a man of fifty, who'd lived through all that. But I came at the half-way stage. I've taken root over there. I've identified myself with too many things. I've got to work to the end of them."

She nodded her head slowly. "I understand," she said. "I think I always did understand." Then, after a pause and with eyes that narrowed, and in a voice that trembled: "Tahiti waits."

But from the deck a bell was ringing. The friends of the passengers were crowding down the ladder; from the taffrail those who were leaving were slowly waving their farewells; the band was playing, the squad of soldiers were presenting arms, the sailors on the lower deck were singing. Slowly, yard by yard, the *Louqsor* drew out into the lagoon, the crowd was drifting from the quay, the tables in the Mariposa Café were filling up, officials were bicycling back to their offices, there was a lazy loitering along the waterside under the gold and scarlet of the flamboyants. A canoe was being launched, some children were bathing in front of Johnnie's. Papeete was returning to its routine. Some friends had come. Some friends had gone. A new day had started.

With a full heart Ray Girling leant over the taffrail. Was he happy or was he sad? He did not know. The strong winds of the Pacific were on his cheeks. He thought of London and his friends; of a life of action; the thrill of business; the stir of ideas and interest. Oh, yes, he would be glad enough to get back to it. But though his blood was beating quicker at the thought, the wreaths of

pandanus and tiare were about his neck, and the sweet, rich
scents were in his nostrils; and before his eyes, in the soft
shadow of a parasol, was a flowerlike face, with eyes that
narrowed; and in his ears was the sound of a voice that
trembled: "Tahiti waits."

LA MARTINIQUE

III

It was while I was on my way to Panama, on my second visit to the South Seas, that I first saw Martinique. Out of a blue sky the sun shone brightly onto a wide square flanked with mango trees, onto yellow houses, onto crowded cafés. And here I thought, maybe, is another and a less far Tahiti. An island in the tropics, under French rule, as far north of the line as was Tahiti south of it. I shall come back here one day, I told myself.

Now, having returned, I am wondering whether it would be possible for two islands to be more different. Their very structure is unlike. They are both mountainous, but whereas the interior of Tahiti is an unpathed, impenetrable jungle, every inch of Martinique is mapped. Nor is West Indian scenery strictly tropical. In Martinique the coconut and the banana are not cultivated systematically. The island's prosperity depends on rum and sugar. And as you drive to Vauclin you have a feeling, looking down from the high mountain roads across fields, green and low-lying, to hidden villages, that you might be in Kent were the countryside less hilly. The aspect of the villages is different. Whereas Tautira is like a garden, with its grass-covered paths, its clean, airy bungalows, its flower-hung verandahs, it is impossible to linger without a feeling of distaste in the dusty, ill-smelling villages of Carbet and Case Pilote, with their dirty, airless cabins, their atmosphere of negligence and squalor. In Tahiti the fishing is done for the most part at night, by the light of torches, on the reef, with spears. In Martinique it is done by day with weighted nets. In Martinique most of the land is owned by a few families. In Tahiti nothing is much harder to discover than the actual proprietor of any piece of ground. Proprietorships have been divided and re-divided, and it is no uncommon thing for a newcomer who imagines that he has completed the purchase of a piece of land to find himself surrounded by a number of claimants, all of whom possess legal right to the ground that their relative has sold him. Scarcely anybody in Tahiti who derives his income from Tahiti has any money. In Martinique there are a number of exceedingly wealthy families. On the other hand, whereas the Tahitian is described as a born millionaire, since he has only to walk up a valley to pick the fruits and spear the fish he needs, the native in Martinique, where every tree and plant exists for the profit of its proprietor, lives in a condition of extreme poverty. The Tahitian woman lives for pleasure. She does hardly any work. By day she lives languidly on her verandah, and by night, with flowers in her hair, she sings and dances and makes love. The woman of Martinique is a beast of burden. When the liner draws up against the quay at Fort de France you will see a crowd of grubby midgets grouped round a bank of coal. When the signal is given they will scurry like ants, with baskets upon their heads, between the ship's tender and the bank of coal. The midgets, every one of them, are women. They receive five sous for every basket that they carry. When there is no ship in port they carry fish and vegetables from the country into town. There is a continual stream of them along every road: dark, erect, hurrying figures bearing, under the heavy sun, huge burdens upon their heads. In Tahiti there exists a small, formal, exclusive French society, composed of a few officials and colonial families, who hold occasional receptions, to which those who commit imprudences are not received. I imagine, at least, that it exists. But the average visitor is unaware of its existence. It is uninfluential. In Martinique, too, there is such a society composed of a few Creole families. It is very formal and very exclusive. Its Sunday *déjeuner* lasts, I am told, till four o'clock. It is also extremely powerful and holds all the power, all the land and most of the money in the island. Tahiti is a pleasure ground; Martinique is a business centre. The atmosphere of Tahiti is feminine; of Martinique masculine. In Fort de France every one is busy doing something: selling cars, buying rum, shipping sugar. Whereas social life in Papeete is complicated by the ramifications of amorous intrigue, in Fort de France it is complicated by the ramifications of politics and commerce. "Life here is a strain," a young dealer said to me. "One has to be diplomatic all the time.

One has business relations of some sort with everybody."
In Papeete it is "affairs" in the English sense; in Fort de
France in the French sense. No one who has not lived in a
small community, each member of whom draws his livelihood from the resources of that country, can realise the
interdependence of all activities, the extent to which
wheels revolve within one another. Every one has some
half-dozen irons in everybody else's grate. In Tahiti the
only people who are in a position to spend money are the
tourists who stay over between two boats and the English and Americans who have come to spend a few months
on the island every year. In Tahiti there is accommodation for the tourist. In Moorea there is a good hotel.
There are bungalows to be let by the month within four
kilometres of Papeete. In the country there are several
places where you can spend a few days in tolerable comfort. In Martinique there are no tourists. Between January and March some dozen English and American liners
stop at St. Pierre. Their passengers drive across the island
to Fort de France, where they rejoin their ship. That is
all. There is no accommodation for the tourist. In Fort
de France there is no hotel where one would spend willingly
more than a few hours. In the country there is no hotel
at all. As far as I could discover there was not in the whole
island a single foreign person who lived there out of choice.
Finally, the native population of Tahiti is freeborn; that
of Martinique has its roots in slavery. You have only to
walk through a native village to realise the difference that
that makes. In Fort de France, which is cosmopolitan,
you do not notice it. But in the country, where day after
day you will not see one white face, you grow more and

more conscious of a hostile atmosphere; you feel it in the glances of the men and women who pass you in the road. When you go into their villages they make you feel that they resent your presence there. You are glad to be past their houses. They will reply to your "Good mornings" and "Good evenings," but they do not smile at you. Often they will make remarks to and after you. They are made in the harsh Creole patois. You do not understand what they say. You suspect that they are insulting you. They are a harsh and sombre people. They do not understand happiness. You will hear them at cock fighting, and at cinemas, shrieking with laughter and excitement, but their faces, whenever they are in repose, are sullen. Their very laughter is strained. They seem to recall still the slavery into which their grandparents were sold. It is only eighty years since slavery was abolished. There are many alive still who have heard from their parents' lips the story of those days: the long journey from Africa, "crowded, terrified and cowed into the pestilent atmosphere of a dark cabin, stagnating between the decks of a Guinea ship, debarred the free use of their limbs, oppressed with chains, harassed with sea sickness and the incessant motions of the vessel, sometimes stinted in provisions and poisoned with corrupted water": afterwards on the plantations there were the chains and lashes. And it is all only eighty years ago. These people have still the mentality of slaves, with only the Australian aborigines below them in the scale of human development. They harbour in their dull brains the heritage of rancour. They are exiles. Under the rich sunlight and the green shadows their blood craves for Africa. They are suspicious with the unceasing animosity of the undeveloped. They cannot believe that they are free. In their own country they were the sport and plunder of their warlike neighbours. It was the easy prey that the pirate hunted. They cannot believe that the white strangers who stole them from their dark cabins have not some further trick to play on them. They cannot understand equality. They will never allow you to feel that you are anywhere but in a land of enemies. In vain will you search through the Antilles for the welcoming friendliness of Polynesia.

§

In Martinique there is no accommodation for the tourists. If you are to stay there you have to become a part of the life of its inhabitants. Within two hours of our arrival Eldred Curwen and I had realised that.

"We have got," we said, "to set about finding a bungalow in the country."

I am told that we were lucky to find a house at all. Certainly we were lucky to find the one we did. Seven kilometres out of town, between Case Navire and Fond Lahaye, a minute's climb from the beach, above the dust of the main road, with a superb panorama of coast line, on one side to Trois Islets, on the other very nearly to Case Pilote, it consisted of three bedrooms, a dining-room, a wide verandah over whose concrete terrace work—the hunting ground of innumerable lizards—trailed at friendly hazard the red and yellow of a rose bush, and the deep purple of the bougainvillea. The stone stairway that ran

84

steep and straight towards the sea was flowered by a green profusion of trees and plants; with bread-fruit, and with papaia; the great ragged branch of the banana; the stately plumes of the bamboo; with far below, latticing the blue of the Caribbean, the slender stem and rustling crest of the coconut palm. It was the kind of house one dreams of, that one never expects to find. Yet nothing could have been found with less expense of spirit.

It was the British Consulate that found it us.

"You want a house," they said. "That is not easy. We will do our best. If you come to-morrow afternoon we will tell you what we have been able to manage."

It was in a mood of no great optimism that we went down there. Every one had shaken their heads when we had told them we were looking for a house.

"Nobody will want to let his house," we had been told. "A house is a man's home. Where would there be for him to go? And for those who have a house both in the country and the town, well, that means that he is a rich man, that his house in the country is his luxury. There are not many luxuries available in the Colonies. He would not be anxious to deprive himself of it."

It sounded logical enough. And when we found two men waiting for us in the Consulate, it was with the expectation of being shown some sorry shack that we followed them into the car. The sight of the house upon the hill was so complete and so delightful a surprise that we would have accepted any rent that its proprietor demanded of us. We were prudent enough, however, to conceal our elation. And three days later we were installed in the bungalow with three comic opera servants, the sum of whose monthly wages in francs can have exceeded only slightly the sum of their united ages.

Our cook, Armantine, received eighty francs. Belmont, the guardian, whose chief duty was the supervision of the water supply and the cutting of firewood, fifty francs. His wife, Florentine, who ran errands, washed plates and did the laundry, had forty francs. It does not sound generous, but it is useless to pay negroes more than they expect. American prosperity is built on a system of high wages. The higher the worker's wages, the higher his standard of living, the higher his purchasing capacity, the greater is the general commercial activity. But the negro in the French Antilles has no ambition; he is quite content with his standard of living. He does not want it raised. If you were to pay him double wages, he would not buy himself a new suit. He would take a month's holiday. A planter once found that however high the wages he offered to the natives, he could not induce them to work. In despair he sought an explanation of an older hand.

"My dear fellow," he was told, "what can you expect with all those fruit trees of yours? Do you think they are going to work eight hours a day when at night they can pick enough fruit to keep them for half a week?"

In the end, at considerable cost and inconvenience, the planter cut down his fruit trees. Then the natives worked.

Our staff considered itself well rewarded with a hundred and seventy francs a month. And it not only made us comfortable but kept us constantly amused.

Armantine was the static element. She was a very adequate cook, considering the limited resources at her disposal. Meat could only be obtained in small quantities twice a week. Lobster was plentiful only when the moon was full. The small white fish was tasteless. There are only a certain number of ways of serving eggs. And yam and bread-fruit, the staple vegetables of the tropics, even when they are flavoured with coconut milk are uninteresting. It says much for her ingenuity that at the end of six weeks we were still able to look forward to our meals. She was also economical. I have little doubt that our larder provisioned her entire family. But no one else was allowed to take advantage of our inexperience. Resolutely, sou by sou, she contested the issue with the local groceries. I should be grateful if in London my housekeeper's weekly books would show no more shillings than Armantine's showed francs. She was also an admirable foil to Florentine.

Florentine was quite frankly a bottle woman. She was never sober when she might be drunk. Amply constructed, I have never seen a person so completely shapeless. Her face was like a piece of unfinished modelling. With her body swathed in voluminous draperies it was impossible to tell where the various sections of it began. When she danced, and she was fond of dancing, she shook like an indiarubber jelly. Very often after dinner when we were playing the gramophone, we would see a shadow slinking along the wall. On realising that its presence had been recognised it would quiver and giggle, turn away its head and produce a mug sheepishly from the intricacies of its raiment. We would look at one another.

"Armantine!" Eldred would call out. "Here!"

In a businesslike, practical manner Armantine hurried round from the kitchen.

"How much," we would ask, "has Florentine drunk to-day?"

Armantine's voice would rise on a crescendo of cracked laughter.

"Too much," she would reply.

We would look sorrowfully at Florentine and shake our heads, and she would shuffle away like a Newfoundland dog that has been denied a bone. On other evenings Armantine would be lenient.

"Yes," she would say, "you may give her some to-night."

So the bottle was got out, the glass was quarter filled. Florentine never looked at the glass while the rum was being poured. She preferred to keep as a surprise the extent of her good fortune, in the same way that a child shuts its eyes till a present is within its hands. And in the same way that a child takes away its present to open it in secret, so would Florentine, with averted face, hurry round the corner of the house. A minute later she would return; a shiny grin across her face.

"Now I will dance for you," she would say.

Sometimes she would become unruly as a result of visits to the village. And Armantine would come to us with a distressed look.

"Please," she would say, "give Florentine some clothes to wash. She earned five francs yesterday. Unless she is employed here, she will go down into the village and get drunk."

So we would make a collection of half-soiled linen, and

sorrowfully Florentine would set about the justifying of her monthly wage.

A grotesque creature, Florentine. But a friendly, and a good-natured one. Once I think she may have been attractive, in a robust, florid, expansive way; the kind of attraction that would be likely to wake a last flicker of enterprise in an ageing heart. For Belmont was very many years her senior. Now he has passed into the kindly harbour of indifference. He does not care what she does. He observes her antics with the same detachment that one accepts the irritating but inevitable excursions of a mosquito. He remains aloof, behind an armour of impressive dignity.

He was one of the most impassive and the most dignified figures that I have ever met. He never hurried. Under the shadow of such a straw hat as one associates with South America he moved at a pace infinitely slower than that of a slow motion film. He possessed a pair of buttonless button boots which can have served no other purpose, so perforated were they, than the warming of his ankles. One day he would wear the right boot. On the next the left. Every fourth or fifth day he would wear neither. Only once did I see him wearing both. That was on New Year's Day. To our astonishment he appeared at breakfast-time in both boots, a straw hat, a flannel shirt buttoned at the neck and a clean white suit. In his hand he carried a bunch of roses. He was going into Fort de France, he explained, to wish the proprietor of the house a happy New Year.

"C'est mon droit," he said, "comme gardien." No

Roman prætor could have boasted more proudly of his citizenship.

Indeed, there was a Roman quality in Belmont. There was something regal about the way he would lean completely motionless for a whole hour against the concrete terrace work, looking out over the sea, and then at the end of the hour walk across to the other side of the verandah to lean there for another hour motionless. And as he slowly climbed the steep stairway from the beach, a long, straight cutlass swinging from his wrist, he looked very like some emperor of the decadence deliberating the execution of a stubborn courtier.

§

There are two ways of forming an impression of a country. In a few weeks one can only hope to gain a first impression. Very often, if one stays longer, the vividness of that first impression goes. The art of reviewing a book is, I am told, not to read the book carefully. Accurate considered judgment of a book within twenty-four hours of reading it is not possible. A rough idea is all that can be got. And it is usually to one's first impression that ultimately one returns. At the end of ten days in a place I have often felt that I should know no more of it if I were to stay ten years, but that were I to stay ten months the clarity of that first impression would be gone. My sight would be confused with detail, I should be unable "to put anything across." The tourist has to rely on first impressions. The question is how is that first impression to be best obtained? There are two ways.

Either you are the explorer, who leaves no corner unexamined, who hurries from place to place collecting and codifying facts; or else you are the observer. From a secluded spot you watch the life of one section of it pass in front of you. From the close scrutiny of that one section you deduce and generalise. Each way has its merits and demerits. It is a matter of temperament, I suppose. Myself, I have always chosen to let life come to me. And in the mornings as I sat on the verandah of our bungalow I had the feeling that I was watching the life of the whole island pass in review before me.

Northwards and southwards, over St. Pierre and Fort de France there is a rainbow curving, for the rainless is as rare as the sunless day; westwards on the horizon beyond "the bright blue meadow of a bay," ships are passing: the stately liners of the Transatlantic, with their twin funnels and their high white superstructures; the smaller boats of three or four thousand tons, the innumerable and homely cargoes, broad, black, low-lying with only the white look-out of the bridge above their high-piled decks. Whither are they bound? Northwards for New York, for Jacmel and the dark republics? Southwards for Cristobal, for the silent wizardry of Panama? Afterwards in the blue Pacific will they turn southwards to Peru, and Ecuador, or northwards to the coffee ports of Mexico and Guatemala; to Champerico, where they haul you in baskets up on to the long iron pier that runs out into the sea; to Puerto Angeles, where the lighters are loaded by hand, by natives who splash through the waves, their broad shoulders loaded; to Manzanillo, where for three intolerable days I sat in the shadow of a café among squabbling Mexicans, while the *City of San Francisco* discharged an oil tank; Salvador, Guatemala, Mexico? In six weeks' time, who knows, these broad beams may be swinging through the Golden Gate, there may be passengers there who six weeks from now will be looking down from the high window of the *St. Francis* onto the lights and animation of the little square. Whither are they bound, those nameless cargoes? Hour after hour I would watch them pass and repass upon the horizon.

Sometimes, in a state of high excitement, Armantine rushed from the kitchen. "Regardez! Tourists Americains!" Slowly, in the majesty of its twenty thousand tons, the vast ship moved southwards. Shortly after breakfast it discharged its passengers at St. Pierre. For a little they wandered among the ruins, then in a fleet of cars they hurried over the Southern road to Fort de France. For an hour or so they will assume control of it. With cameras in their hands they will stroll through the town as though it were an exhibition. They will peer into private houses. They will load themselves with souvenirs, with shouts of laughter they will call each other's attention to such sights as will appear to them remarkable. They will consider fantastically humorous their attempts to make themselves understood in pidgeon French. For an hour, buying, examining, commenting, they will parade the town. Then, with a sigh of relief, they will consider their educational duty to themselves acquitted. It is time the fun began.

"Let's go some place and enjoy ourselves," they say.

As likely as not they will choose the Café Bediat. It is lunch time. But they do not bother about food. You can eat anywhere. You can eat in Ogden and Omaha and Buffalo. You do not come all the way to Martinique to eat.

"Rhum; compris rhum? Beaucoup," they will tell the waitresses.

There is no nonsense about their drinking. They do not spoil good liquor with ice or lime or syrup. This isn't bootleg gin. They know how to treat the real stuff when they meet it. They take it straight. A port glass of neat rum in the one hand, a tumblerful of ice water as a chaser in the other, they set about the serious business of their trip. By the time the last syren of their steamer goes half the men and three quarters of the women are drunk. In a country where you can drink all you want for two francs and as much as you can carry for four, they toss their hundred franc notes upon the table.

"Ah, don't bother about that," they say, as the waitress fumbles in her pocket. "If you can find any use for that flimsy pink stuff, you cling on to it."

Laughing and shouting, arm in arm, they sway towards the ship, having in one small section of the globe done their country's name more damage in four hours than her statesmen and engineers and artists can do it good in as many years. To-morrow they will pass the day comparing "hang-overs." Who are these people, what are they, where do they come from? In America itself one never sees them.

§

Far on the horizon the large ships pass; the liners, the tourists, and the cargoes. Nearer the shore is the little tug that plies between St. Pierre and Fort de France. It carries mail and cargo and a few passengers, stopping at Belfontain and Carbet and Case Pilote. At Carbet there is a little pier against which the tug is wharfed. But at Belfontain and Case Pilote and St. Pierre small boats row out to it. A fierce conflict is always staged about the ladder. The boat that gets its cargo and passengers discharged first will get back to the shore in time for another load. No sooner has a boat got into position beside the ladder than another boat enfilades it, creeping closer to the side of the ship; it tries to elbow it out into the sea. It is a form of aquatic spillikins: the object of the game being to displace the other boat without upsetting its passengers and cargoes into the water. The sailors shriek at each other like base-ball players. It is a damp and noisy game. The last time I made such an excursion I offered our boatman double fare if he would wait till last. He shook his head. The game was greater than the reward.

Four or five times a day the little tug passes across the bay. And between it and the shore are always a number of fishing boats. For the most part in Martinique they fish with nets. The nets are long and about ten feet deep. One side of the nets is strung with cork, the other is weighted. Two canoes, rowing outwards from one another, swing the net into a circle. To bring the fish to the surface they throw stones into the circle and beat the water with their oars. Then gradually, foot by foot, they draw in the nets.

They are small fish for the greater part and most of them are sent into the market at Fort de France. From my verandah in the morning, I watch the girls coming over the hill from Fond Lahaye, carrying baskets of them upon their heads. In one of his loveliest essays Lafcadio Hearn has described the life of "La Porteuse": the girl who is, in comparison with the Charbonière, as is the race horse to the cart horse; who for thirty francs a month travelled her thirty miles a day, who was trained from childhood to her profession, whose speed was so fast that an averagely strong walker could not keep pace with her for fifteen minutes. In those days all the trade of the island was in her hands. But it was forty years ago that Hearn lived under the shadow of Mont Pelée; to-day the truck and the lorry have taken the place very largely of "La Porteuse." The big plantations have no need for her. It is only from the small estates and the fishing villages that morning after morning the young island women are sent out, their heads laden, into Fort de France. In a few years "La Porteuse" will have vanished. But the sight of those slim, upright, exquisitely proportioned girls moving in a smooth, fast stride under their heavy loads is still one of the most picturesque features of the island.

Now and again one or other of them pauses in the roadway below the bungalow.

"Armantine!" she calls out, "I have fish."

We sign to her to come up, and without the least appearance of effort she climbs the long, steep flight to lay down her charge on the top step of the verandah. Usually it is a basket of small fish. And nothing is more deceptive than the small fish of the tropics. There they lie, an infinite variety of shapes and colours. In appearance no two of them are the same; but in taste they are identical. And their taste is that of dry bread that has been soaked in water. When the moon is full or waxing, however, it is the langouste that she brings. Then the entire bungalow is stirred into interest. We all gather round the verandah steps: Eldred, myself, Armantine and Florentine. Even Belmont now and again, with a small three months' pig trotting at his heels. We stand in a semicircle, looking at the basket.

"How much?" says Eldred. "That, the little one."

For here, as in Europe, the taste of the small langouste is delicate.

The girl lifts it up by its tendrils. She examines carefully its flicking tail. "Five francs," she says. We roar with laughter. "Five francs!" we say. "We bought a far better one than that for four francs yesterday." The girl turns away her head and the inevitable bargaining begins. Sou by sou we approach a central figure. In the end we get the lobster for four francs fifty. The days are few on which somebody does not bring us something: bread-fruit or coconut or bananas. Once there was a rabbit and once a hare.

Sometimes, sitting quietly on my verandah, I felt that in the course of a day I had seen the whole life of the island pass in front of me. Far on the horizon there are the big ships, the liners and the cargoes that maintain contact between it and the world, that bring to it the blood that feeds it: the fabric and machinery it needs; that in exchange carry away the rum and sugar that make it rich. And, closer, there is the little tug plying between St. Pierre and Fort de France, that maintains contact between the various island villages that hill and stream separate from one another. And still nearer, between the tug's path and the shore, are the fishing boats on which rests the prosperity of those villages, and along the road there are the young girls carrying that produce to its consumer, and on my verandah there is the salesmanship and the unit of exchange.

The whole life of the island in a day.

§

"I suppose," said Eldred at the end of our second day at Case Navire, "that sooner or later we shall find the snag to this."

We never did. Day after day life followed its happy and unexacting course. No routine could have been simpler. In the tropics it is light by six. And before the tug that leaves Fort de France at daybreak had turned the headland beyond Fond Lahaye I was drinking my morning coffee. By seven I was at work. I remained there for four hours. In London, where one is surrounded by distractions, by the noises in the streets, by telephones, by the morning's post, by one's conversation of the previous evening, by the thought of the party one is going to that night, it is only by the most rigid seclusion that one can hope to concentrate upon one's work. But in the tropics, where there are no distractions, where there are no telephones, no letters, no conversations to remember or look forward to, you welcome the casual interruptions of an island day. You are content enough to hear a gramophone playing behind your shoulder, to discuss in the middle of a paragraph the menu for the day's meal and the extent of Armantine's weekly books; to exchange gossip with

97

Belmont and join in the friendly bargaining round the lobster basket. At eleven I would put away my books, shave, and go to join Eldred Curwen, who would be sunbathing on the beach. It was in a very secluded, shut in, and unobserved section of the beach that we bathed; so secluded that we thought bathing clothes unnecessary. It cannot, however, have been as secluded as we thought, for one morning we found chalked upon our cabin: "They are bathing necked just like worms. Dirty peoples!" We left the writing there, and one evening, a few days later, we found a studious half caste standing in front of it turning the pages of a pocket dictionary. His face wore a puzzled look.

At half-past twelve we lunched. And with lunch the bad period in the tropical day has started. It is very hot. One's eyes are dazzled by the glare. Most people prefer to go to bed. If you have eaten heavily and taken alcohol at lunch no power on earth can keep your eyelids open if you lie out on a long chair. Most Europeans do siesta, but myself, I have never felt anything but the worse for one. You wake as you do after a heavy night. Even a shower does not put you straight. And invariably that hour or so of sleep ruins your night's rest. Myself, I have always found that it is better to lunch lightly, to avoid alcohol till sundown, and after lunch to write letters, play chess or patience; at any rate, to choose an occupation that demands the sitting erect on a hard chair. By three o'clock the worst is over. One is ready for a walk.

I am told that it is dangerous in the tropics to take much exercise. But I have been told that so many things are dangerous in the tropics. I have been told that unless I

98

wore coloured glasses I should get sunstroke through the eyes, and that without a sun helmet through the head. I have been told that if I ate lettuce I should get dysentery; that if I did not eat green vegetables I should catch scurvy. I was told that I should catch elephantiasis by going barefoot. I have been told that unless I wore underclothes I should catch a skin complaint called "dobiage." I have been told that alcohol is poison, and that whiskey is the only antidote to malaria. Each particular part of the tropics has its particular fad. The French wear sun helmets eighteen degrees north of the equator; the English wear underclothes on the equator. We all have our fads. Mine is, I suppose, the refusal to take a siesta after lunch. Anyhow, I have always felt better on the days when, in addition to two good swims, I have done an eight-mile walk.

And there are good walks in Martinique. Even if the roads are appalling the countryside is varied. One section of it is pasture ground. Another is laid out in sugar. There are coconut groves by Carbet. In the extreme south there is practically a desert, where you can find the prickly pear. While high on Balata, in imitation of Montmartre, there is the Sacre Cœur of Martinique, a vast white church that you can see from half the island. There is no lack of walks in Martinique. And by the time that one is back the best hour of the day has started. The sun is low in the sky; there is no glare from the sea nor from the red stone of the verandah; the green of the hills takes on a deeper, almost an unreal, green: though really it is for that hour only during the day that you see their true colouring. When the sun is high their burnished surfaces

99

are no more than mirrors. It is only in that last hour of daylight that you can realise the incredible deepness of their colouring.

And later, after we had bathed, after the sun had sunk, a rapid red descent into the sea, we would lie out on the verandah in deck chairs, with the violet of the sky darkening and the crickets and lizards beginning to murmur from the hills. We should not talk a great deal. We should be listening with strained ears for the sound of a Rugby's horn. Our only means of communication with Fort de France was a car, a kind of private bus garaged in Case Navire, that carried a passenger or two each morning, ran errands in town, and in the evening brought out a load of passengers and such provisions as might have been ordered by its clients. It was on this car that we relied for our ice, for our bread and for our butter. We never knew when the car would arrive nor how much would have been forgotten. The ice usually appeared. The bread two days in three; the butter perhaps one in four. It was like waiting for rations to arrive during the War. And till the ice had arrived, till the decanter of rum and sugar had been set out, we could not settle down to the peace of a tropic evening, than which I have found nothing in the world more lovely and serene.

Sometimes friends from Fort de France would join us. Suddenly, at about seven o'clock, there would be the hooting of a horn, the flash of lights along a drive, and up the steps a shouting of "We've brought some ice; and some new Sophie Tucker records. So we're hoping that we'll be welcome."

These visits were always unexpected; such visits always are in Martinique. During our first weeks we invited people for fixed days, made preparation and kept meals back for them. But we soon learnt that in Martinique, when people say "We will come out on Wednesday," they usually mean "some time in the middle of the week." So after a while we said, just vaguely, "Come out when you'ld like a bathe." And sometimes they did and sometimes they didn't. And when they did it simply meant the adding of an egg or two to the omelette or the opening of another tin. And we would bathe and chatter and play the new Sophie Tucker records and dance on the balcony in a moon-silvered dusk. But whether friends came out or not, by half-past ten the bungalow was quiet and asleep

§

Into Fort de France we went as rarely as possible. For that is about the first thing that travel teaches one: that life in a town is just not possible. Of the many tropical towns that I have visited, Penang is the only one in which I should be happy to make a home. It would be surprising, indeed, if it were otherwise. The population of every tropical town is either commercial or administrative. Every one has a definite reason for being there. There is no leisured class to create an interior world that exists for its own amusement. Since the majority of such towns are of recent growth, there are no interesting buildings, no picture galleries to be seen. In consequence, there is absolutely nothing for the unoccupied tourist to do till offices close at five o'clock and companionship is again at his disposal.

Fort de France was no exception. It is a pretty town. From the balcony of the club you look out over the green stretch of the Savane. On your left is a flanking of yellow houses; to your right the blue water of the harbour, the masts of schooners, the red funnels of cargo boats and liners. In front of you, circled by sentinel palms, is the white statue of Josephine, her face turned southwards to the Trois Isles, where she was born. Fort de France is easily the prettiest town in the Leeward and Windward groups, and it was charitable of fate to divert northwards the cyclone that in the autumn of 1928 raged over the Antilles. At Guadeloupe there was little that can not be rebuilt. And over Guadeloupe the cyclone raged very mercilessly.

"Heaven knows how we shall get into port to-morrow," said the captain of the *Pellerin* on the eve of our arrival. "I don't know what there'll be to recognise it by."

Yet, when we did arrive, Pointe à Pitre seemed very little different from the picture that my memory had formed of it. I had only spent a day and a night there on my way towards Panama, but those few hours had left an ineffaceable impression of dejected squalor. With its straight, puddle-spotted streets, its wooden and tin houses, garnished with slipshod balconies, it always looked as though it were about to fall to pieces. It reminded me of the kind of small town in an early Keystone comedy, that was destined every inch of it to be knocked down in the last hundred feet of film. The cyclone, instead of altering Pointe à Pitre, seemed to have put it in harmony with itself. In the same way that when you set side by side a photograph of a landscape and a modern painting of it you say of the photograph. "That's what it looks like," and of the painting, "That's what it really is"; so as I walked through Pointe à Pitre, remembering Pointe à Pitre as it had been sixteen months earlier, as I paused before the battered houses, the piles of masonry and iron, the spreadeagled balconies, the uprooted trees, the twisted bandstand, the unroofed and unclocked cathedral, onto whose floor through innumerable apertures the rain was pouring; "Yes," I kept saying to myself, of this melancholy provincial town through which the business of life in market and shop and office was continuing in unaltering indolence, "this is how it really is."

It was not till we got out of Pointe à Pitre into the country that we realised what the cyclone had really meant. The effect there was extraordinary. The countryside, with its coconut palms lopped and uprooted, gave the impression of a face that has not been shaved for several days. Like a blunt razor the cyclone had passed over it. As I drove through the wrecked landscape towards Basseterre I thanked Heaven very humbly that it had spared the green Savane, and the white statue and the palm trees guarding it; that in all its beauty and friendliness Fort de France should be waiting there untouched to welcome me.

And yet, lovely though it is, Fort de France is intolerably hot. Set in a basin of hills, its very excellencies as a harbour make it the less habitable. Not a breath of air reaches it. Every one who can afford to, lives out of town, in the cool and quiet of the hills. Not only is Fort de France extremely hot, it is also very noisy. The streets are narrow, the cars are many. The chauffeurs drive with the recklessness, but not the skill, of Parisian taximen. When cars were introduced into Northern Siam the sense of speed was so intoxicating to the Laos that in Chiengmai artificial bumps were raised in the main streets to force the chauffeur to drive slowly. I have often wished, as I have seen disaster approaching me at every corner, that the authorities in Fort de France would take the same precautions. But it is doubtful if it would have much effect. If the roads were as bumpy as the scenic railway in San Francisco, I think that the Martiniquaises would continue to rush their fences, trusting blindly in the immunity of one-way streets and a hand rhythmically pressed upon a horn. All the time horns are honking. It is one's last, it is one's first, impression of Fort de France. Long before evening one's head has begun to ache.

The casual traveller, with nothing definite to occupy him finds his attention concentrated exclusively on the incessant noise. Only during the week-ends is there systematised entertainment.

§

Every Sunday morning there was cock-fighting. It was worth seeing once. The Gallodrome was a circular wooden building, arranged in five galleries. On the top gallery there was a piano and a bar. You paid five francs at the door. The pit was about twenty feet across. For the first minute and a half a fight is thrilling. The cocks are introduced to one another by their owners: they are placed on the edge of a circle five feet apart. The instant they are let loose they fly at one another. Quite often in that first leap, with a single blow, one of them is killed. For a moment or two it is a whirlwind of blows and feathers. But after that minute it grows uninteresting. The cocks do not, as in the North of England, wear spurs. They peck wearily at the back of each other's necks. The chief interest is in the audience: in the half-castes and negroes who bounce excitedly in their seats, who shriek encouragement to the animals, who shout their odds across the pit.

Nominally the fight is to the death; actually it is as long as the cocks will fight. After a quarter of an hour or so they stand, blind and weary, gasping and indifferent, the fight forced out of them. Their owners take them by the wings and place them at the edge of the circle, facing each other, five feet apart. They make no movement. Inside that circle there is a smaller circle. Again the animals are lifted by their wings. They are within a few inches now of one another. They do not move. The crowd yells fiercely. Then suddenly one pecks forward. The other turns away its head. The fight is finished. Pandemonium is released. The negroes jump in their seats and shriek with excitement, waving the francs that they have lost or won, while the owners carry away the cocks, scrape the skins of their heads and legs with a small pocket knife, slit the congested flesh about the neck and crown, pour lemon juice over the wounds, and hope for equal or greater fortune in the following week.

Within five minutes another fight has started.

Cock-fighting is the chief sport in Martinique. Every district has its fight on Sunday.

In the villages there are no cock-pits. The negroes

form a rough circle round the cocks, and as the fight moves the circle follows up and down the length of the village street. From a distance it looks like a scrum in Rugby football. Children perch themselves on verandahs and on the roofs of cabins; they shriek with laughter when the cocks fall into a gutter or stumble over a more than ordinarily misplaced cobblestone. It is a hilarious business. But to see cock-fighting at its best you have to see it at the three big centres, at Trinité, St. Pierre and Fort de France. In the same way that, although there is a Festa of some sort in every village on the six or seven Sundays before Lent, to see carnival at its best you have got to go to Fort de France.

§

For the actual carnival I was at Dominica. And there it was a subdued affair. Two years earlier there had been trouble, a police officer had been beaten very nearly to death. Dominica is a curious place. Once a French possession and geographically a French possession still, it is in feeling more French than English. It is Roman Catholic. The natives speak Creole. Smuggling, that the police are powerless to check, is constantly carried on between Martinique and Guadeloupe. Dominica is the Ireland of the Antilles. It is the loveliest of the islands, and it is the most difficult to manage. It should be prosperous, but blight after blight has fallen on the crops. First coffee was destroyed. Then when the lime industry was established—Dominica is the centre of Rose's lime juice—a disease struck that. The country is very moun-

106

tainous. When Columbus was asked to describe the island he crumpled up a sheet of paper and tossed it on the table. The roads are so bad that fruit cannot be profitably marketed. Dominica is a constant drain on the Imperial Government's exchequer. The more money that is spent there, the less settled does life become. Anything might have happened in Roseau during that wild week of carnival had not a gunboat providentially and unexpectedly arrived in harbour. Many stories are told in explanation of that gunboat's presence. It is said that an admiral expressed a wish for grape fruit. There was no grape fruit, he was told. Where could grape fruit be got? Nowhere nearer than Dominica. Could any excuse be devised for sending a gunboat there? Papers were consulted, an American courier had passed two days before. There might be a mail there. That was sufficient excuse when an admiral was hungry. And so at the very moment when Roseau was in the hands of the rebels a gunboat appeared in the harbour. There was no fighting. The crowds dispersed, the sailors were not even aware that there had been any trouble. The sight of the gunboat was enough. In five minutes order had been restored. That evening the admiral ate grape fruit before *consommé*.

Probably the story is untrue. But the arrival of the gunboat was no less providential on that account. In the following year the carnival was forbidden. And when I was there, though the carnival took place, no sticks were carried, and at six o'clock the streets were cleared. It was an orderly affair. It lasted for two days. In the morning from the hour of nine the streets were patrolled by small groups of men and women with masks and costumes, a drum at their head, at their back a crowd of ecstatic urchins. The costumes were as various as the local store and local wit permitted. There were pierrots and pierrettes, there were sailors and there were cowboys, there were men dressed as women, padded with footballs to give their skirts the effect of a Victorian bustle. Some tried to make themselves appear attractive, the majority tried to make themselves as plain as possible. In Fort de France there were occasional satirists. One afternoon a group of men, dressed up as women in skirts five inches long, had paraded the streets singing "Malpropre baissez la robe." Most of the songs that are sung at carnival are impromptu references to some local event. The chief song at Roseau commemorated an attempted suicide.

"Sophia drink wine and iodine
Why, why, Sophia?"

During the afternoon Roseau echoed the name Sophia. Every shop was shut. Half the population was "running mask." The stray groups that had shouted down the streets during the morning had joined up into a solid phalanx, seventy yards in length, that marched backwards and forwards, singing and dancing, cracking whips; while separate bands of twenty to a dozen girls, dressed uniformly, marched with small orchestras to solicit alms. Each band represented something. One band dressed in yellow represented Colman's mustard, another *Tit-bits*, a third, hung with red, white and blue, carrying plates of oranges and maize and bread-fruit, "Dominica Produce." It was the Martinique carnival on a small scale, exceeded by it in the same way that in its turn Martinique is exceeded by Trinidad. If you want to see street carnival go to Port of Spain. But if you want to see that of which street carnival is the symbol you will stay in Fort de France. In white-run sections of the world I never expect to see a more astounding exhibition than the Bal Lou-Lou.

Twice a week, on Saturdays and Sundays, there is a ball, or rather there are several. There is the Palais and the Casino. But it is at the Select Tango that you will see it at its best. There is nothing to tell you that you are to see anything extraordinary. At the end of a quiet street facing a river there is a large tin building. You pay your twelve francs and you are in a long room hung with lanterns and paper streamers. A gallery runs round it, on which tables are set, and at each of whose extremities there is a bar. It is rather like a drill-hall. And as you lean over the balcony you have the impression that you are at a typical provincial palais de danse. You see the kind of people that you would expect to see. On the gallery there are one or two family parties of white people. The white women will not dance. They will look on, and they will leave early. In the hall below are a certain number of young Frenchmen of good family with their dusky mistresses. There will be some white policemen and white soldiers; but for the most part it is a coloured audience of shop assistants, minor officials, small proprietors; a typical provincial dance hall. And at first in the dance itself there is nothing that you would not expect to see in such a place. The music is more barbaric, more gesticulatory; but that you would expect to find. As the evening passes, as the custom at the bar grows busier, the volume of sound increases, but that, too, you would expect. That

you have seen before. You grow tired and a little bored.
You begin to wonder whether it is worth staying on. Then
suddenly there is the wail of a clarionet. A whisper
runs round the tables: "Danse du pays." In a moment
the galleries are empty.

It is danced face to face. The girl clasps her arms round
the man's neck. The man holds her by the hips. The
music is slow and tense. "Le talent pour la danseuse,"
wrote Moreau St. Mery, "est dans la perfection avec
laquelle elle peut faire mouvoir ses hanches et la partie
inferieure des ses reins en conservant tout le reste du corps
dans un espèce d'immobilité." The couples appear scarcely
to move. In a dance of twenty minutes they will not make
more than one revolution of the room. They stand, close
clasped and swaying. The music does not grow louder or
more fast. It grows fiercer, more barbaric. The mouths
of the dancers grow lax; their eyes are clouded, their
movements exceed symbol. "La danse s'arrive et beintot
elle offre un tableau dont tout les traits d'abord volup-
tueux deviennent ensuite laxifs. Il serait impossible de
peindre la *chica* [1] avec son veritable caractère et je me bor-
nerai a dire que l'impression qu'elle fait est si puissante que
l'africain ou le Creole de n'importe quelle nuance qui le
verrait danser sans emotion passerait pour avoir perdu
jusqu'aux dernières étincelles de la sensibilité."

That is on ordinary evenings. During carnival it is
fantastic. A stranger arriving at the Select Tango at one
o'clock in the morning would imagine himself mad. He
would not believe it possible that in a white-run com-

---

[1] The actual *chica* is a slightly different dance, somewhat similar to the Hula-Hula.
The couples do not touch each other as they dance.

munity the payment of twelve francs at a public turnstile would admit him to such a Bedlam. He would imagine that such spectacles were held behind doors as rigidly guarded as those of the Bal des Quartre Arts. The noise is deafening. The galleries and hall are crowded. Most of the girls are masked. They wear gloves and stockings so that not an inch of dark skin appears. Some of them, it is whispered, are white women in disguise. They might well be. It is a dance in which caste and blood are alike forgotten. Every one is drunk; not with alcohol, but with music. People are dancing by themselves. They shriek and wave their arms. They seize a partner, dance with her for a moment, then break away. A girl will be dancing by herself. "Un danseur s'approche d'elle, s'élance tout à coup et tombe au mesure presque à la toucher. Il recule. Il s'élance encore, et la provoque à la lutte la plus seduisante." The young Frenchmen in the arms of their mulatto mistresses will parody and exaggerate the antics of the negroes. A woman embraced between two men will be shrieking to friends up on the gallery. In the thronged centre of the ball couples close-clasped will stand swaying, their feet and shoulders motionless, a look of unutterable ecstasy upon their faces.

But it is not possible to describe the Bal Lou-Lou. The only phrases that would describe it are incompatible with censorship.

§

Once every five days or so we went into Fort de France, and it was always with a feeling of excitement that we began the day. It was fun after five days of bare legs and open throats to put on trousers and arrange a tie. The seven-kilometre drive assumed the proportion of high adventure; which in point of fact, with a chauffeur such as ours, it was. We felt very like country cousins coming up for a day's shopping as we deposited with the head waiter of the Hotel de la Paix a list of groceries and a vast wooden box in which to store them. There was the excitement of discovering at the photographer's how many of the snapshots we had taken during the previous weeks were recognisable comments on the landscape. And by the time that was finished it would be half-past eleven.

"The club," Eldred would remark, "will probably not be empty now."

There was a delightfully welcoming friendliness about the club. There would be certain to be four or five of our friends on the wide, airy verandah looking out over the Savane. We would draw our chairs up into the circle. Hands would be clasped, decanters would be set upon the table. There would be silence while the waitress performed the ritual of mixing a Creole punch: quarter of a finger's height of sugar, two fingers high of rum, the paring of a lime, the rattling of ice. Then talk would begin, friendly, unexacting gossip, the exchange of comment and reminiscence, till the hands of the clock were pointing at half-past twelve, with the world, after a couple of rum punches, appearing a pretty companionable place.

"We ought to come into town more often," we would say as we hurried lunchwards, down the Rue Perignon. And after five days of eggs and lobster and native vegetables it was fun to eat a chateau-briand that you would certainly not be grateful for in London, and drink a *vin ordinaire* with which even in a New York speakeasy the management would hesitate to serve you. And, "Certainly, we must come in more often," we would say as we sat over our coffee afterwards on the terrace of the hotel. But it would be no more than half-past one when we would be saying that. And the sun was beating fiercely upon the corrugated iron of the roof; in the street below the cars were honking merrily. For three and a half hours the club was certain to be empty. There was nothing for us to do. We could go to the gramophone shop, of course, and play some tunes. But you cannot stay more than an hour in a shop where you are only going to buy one record and the last two numbers of "La Sourire." And even an hour leaves you with two and a half hours to be killed. There is the library, of course, and it is a good library. But the heat and the noise make concentration difficult. Usually it ended in a visit to the Delices du Lido.

"At any rate," we'ld say, "it'll be cool and quiet there." Whatever the Delices might not be, on days when there was no boat in it was that.

The actual town of Fort de France is about half a mile from the coaling station; a road shadowed by a tent of trees curves round an inlet of the bay to the Savane; on the left of the road, on boat days, are innumerable vendors of fruit and cakes; on the right a collection of two-storey wooden houses. It is to this that sailors refer when they tell you that Martinique is the loveliest island they have ever seen. It is the only part of the island that most of them ever do see. It is the red light district.

And it is, beyond question, the most picturesque part of the town. At sunset the view across the bay is the loveliest thing I have seen this side of the canal. And in the afternoon even, the Delices du Lido is about the most pleasant place in the town to sit about in. By the time we left the island we had come to know the majority of the girls there. They were mulattoes—when they were not pure negresses,—simple, smiling, friendly and improvident; laughing and chattering, quarrelling and crying. The kind of girls that one would expect to find in such a place. There was one girl, however, whose presence there was inexplicable. She was one of the ten loveliest women that I have ever seen. She was very young. She could not have been more than twenty. Seeing her in Martinique, one knew that she must have coloured blood in her; but if one had met her in Paris or London one would not have suspected it. She was of the Spanish type. Her features had genuine refinement. Good clothes and a good hairdresser would have made her the kind of woman whose entrance into a London restaurant would have meant the turning of twenty heads. I do not see how in any big town a girl with her appearance would not have been a big success. Yet, here she was in this wretched stew, the associate of lascars and third mates.

What was she doing there? How had she got there? Why was she staying there? They were questions to which I could find no answer. As long as she remained there she was futureless. No man would run the risk of taking her away from such an atmosphere. Sometimes I wondered whether she did not enjoy the sense of superiority that she could exert in such a place. She was by no means an agreeable person. She was arrogant and disdainful; she never hid her contempt for the other girls, on whom she was constantly making cruel and cutting remarks. Such a one might relish the sense of empire that such a setting gave her. Probably, though, that is too involved an explanation. Probably her presence in that one-way street meant nothing more than that she was lazy. It was a problem, whose fascination led us most afternoons to the ordering of a series of lime squashes in the Delices du Lido. But though Fort de France could offer no better entertainment to the tourist, it was an unsatisfactory one.

For soft drinks do you no more good than rum does in the afternoon. You are better without either. I have never spent an afternoon in Fort de France without envying those who had offices and telephones, letters to be dictated and strings of agents trying to ship their sugar crops. I have never at the day's end, without a feeling of unutterable relief, looked down from the climbing road on to the lighted streets and the lights of the ships at anchor.

One such day in particular I remember. We had come into Fort de France one afternoon, in the mistaken belief that a friend of Eldred's was on the *Flandre*. We had spent a hot and profitless half hour walking round an oven-like ship. Coaling was in progress and the coal dust had blown into our eyes and mouths. We were hot, fractious, and uncomfortable. "Let's go and have an orangeade and then get out of this as quickly as possible," we said. On the steps of the club, however, we ran into the son of its President, Edouard Boulenger.

"What, you fellows here?" he said. "You're just in time. Jump in quick. We're going up to the pit. There's a fight on. A snake and a mongoose."

It was the first time that I had seen such a fight.

There is not actually a great deal to see. It is darkish inside the building, the pit itself is netted over, and through the mesh of wire it is hard to distinguish against the brown sanded floor the movements of the small dark forms. You see a brown line along the sand and a brown shadow hovering. Then suddenly there is a gleam of white; the thrashing of the snake's white belly. For a few moments the brown shadow is flecked with the twisting and writhing of the white whip. Then the brown shadow slinks away. The *fer de lance,* the most hostile small snake in the world, is still. There is not a great deal to see. But it is thrilling. There is a taut, tense atmosphere, not only through the fight, but afterwards when the snake has been lifted out of the pit, while its head is cut open and the poison poured into a phial. During a cock-fight there is an incessant noise. Every one shouts and gesticulates. But there is complete silence during the snake's silent battle. It has a sinister quality. And it is with a feeling of exhaustion and of relief that you come out into the street, into the declining sunlight. You are grateful for the sound of voices.

Longer than usual that evening we sat on the verandah of the club. It was completely dark when we came down its stairs into the Savane. Never had the cool and quiet of the hills been more welcome. Never had a bathe seemed a completer banishment of every harassing circumstance that the day had brought. Low in the sky there was a moon, a baby moon. As we swam it was half moonshine and half phosphorus, the splintered silver that was about us. And even in the north of Siam, after a day of marching over precipitous mountain paths and above flooded paddy fields, I have known no peace more utter than the lying out on the verandah after dinner, watching the moon and the Southern Cross sink side by side into the sea, hearing from every bush and shrub the murmur of innumerable crickets.

§

Once we went to St. Pierre.

From Ford Lahaye it is a three hours' sail in a canoe, along a coast indented with green valleys that run back climbingly through fields of sugar cane. At the foot of most of these valleys, between the stems of the coconut palms, you see the outline of wooden cabins. So concealed are these cabins behind that façade of greenery that were it not for the fishing nets hung out along the beach on poles to dry you would scarcely suspect that there was a village there. Nor, as you approach St. Pierre, would you suspect that in that semicircle of hills under the cloud-hung shadow of Mont Pelée, are hidden the ruins of a city for which history can find no parallel.

At first sight it is nothing but a third-rate, decrepit shipping port, not unlike Manzanillo or La Libertad. It has its pier, its warehouses, its market; its single cobbled street contains the usual dockside features. A café or two, a restaurant, a small wooden shanty labelled "Cercle," a somewhat larger shanty labelled "Select Tango." A hair-dresser, a universal store. At first sight it is one of many

119

thousand places. It is not till you step out of that main street into the tangled jungle at the back of it that you realise that St. Pierre is, as it has always been, unique.

Even then you do not at first realise it. At first you see nothing but greenery, wild shrubbery, the great ragged leaves of the banana plant, with here and there the brown showing of a thatched roof. It is not till you have wandered a little through those twisted paths that you see that it is in the angles of old walls that those thatched cottages are built, that it is over broken masonry, over old stairways and porticoes, that those trailing creepers are festooned; the empty windows are shadowed by those ragged leaves. At odd corners you will come upon signs of that old life: a marble slab that was once the doorstep of a colonial bungalow; a fountain that splashed coolly through siestaed summers; a shrine with the bronze body broken at its foot. Everywhere you will come upon signs of that old life; *le pays des revenants*, they called it. With what grim irony has chance played upon the word.

But it is not till you have left the town and have climbed to the top of one of the hills that were thought to shelter it, till you look down into the basin of the amphitheatre that contained St. Pierre, and, looking down, see through the screen of foliage the outline of house after ruined house, that you realise the extent and nature of the disaster. No place that I have ever seen has moved me in quite that way.

Not so much by the thought of the twenty-eight thousand people killed within that narrow span: to the actual fact of death most of us are, I think, now a little callous. Nor by the sentiment that attaches itself to any ruin, the sentiment with which during the war one walked through the deserted villages of Northern France, the feeling that here a life that was the scene of many lives has been abandoned; that here, at the corners of these streets, men had stood gossiping on summer evenings, watching the sky darken over the unchanging hills, musing on the permanence, the unhurrying continuity of the life they were a part of. It is not that sentiment that makes the sight of St. Pierre so profoundly solemn. It is the knowledge rather that here existed a life that should be existing still, that existed nowhere else, that was the outcome of a combination of circumstances that now have vanished from the world for ever. Even Pompeii cannot give you quite that feeling. There were many Pompeiis, after all. Pompeii exists for us as a symbol, as an explanation of Roman culture. It has not that personal, that localised appeal of a flower that has blossomed once only, in one place: that no eye will ever see again.

St. Pierre was the loveliest city in the West Indies. The loveliest and the gayest. All day its narrow streets were bright with colour; in sharp anglings of light the amber sunshine streamed over the red tiled roofs, the lemon-coloured walls, the green shutters, the green verandahs. The streets ran steeply, "breaking into steps as streams break into waterfalls." Moss grew between the stones. In the runnel was the sound of water. There was no such thing as silence in St. Pierre. There was always the sound of water, of fountains in the hidden gardens, of rain water in the runnels, and through the music of that water, the water that kept the town cool during the long noon heat, came ceaselessly from the hills beyond the murmur of the lizard and the cricket. A lovely city, with its theatre, its lamplit avenues, its *jardin des plants*, its schooners drawn circlewise along the harbour. Life was comely there; the life that had been built up by the old French *emigrés*. It was a city of carnival. There was a culture there, a love of art among those people who had made their home there, who had not come to Martinique to make money that they could spend in Paris. The culture of Versailles was transposed there to mingle with the Carib stock and the dark mysteries of imported Africa. St. Pierre was never seen without emotion. It laid hold of the imagination. It had something to say, not only to the romantic intellectual like Hearn or Stacpoole, but to the sailors and the traders, to all those whom the routine of livelihood brought within the limit of its sway. "Incomparable," they would say as they waved farewell to the Pays des Revenants, knowing that if they did not return they would carry all their lives a regret for it in their hearts.

History has no parallel for St. Pierre.

And within forty-five seconds the stir and colour of that life had been wiped out.

The story of the disaster is too familiar, has been told too many times to need any retelling here. The story of those last days when Pelée was scattering cinders daily over Martinique; when the vegetables that the women brought down from the hills to market were dark with ashes; when the Rivière Blanche was swollen with boiling mud; when day after day was darkened by heavy clouds: it has been told so often, the story of that last morning that dawned clear after a night of storm for the *grande fête* of an Ascension Day: of the two immense explosions that were heard clearly in Guadeloupe, of the voice over a telephone abruptly silenced, of the ship that struggled with charred and corpse-strewn deck into the harbour of Saint Lucia, the ship that two years later was to be crushed by ice: of the voice that cried back to the questioner on the wharf, "We come from Hell. You can cable the world that St. Pierre exists no longer." It has been told so many times.

At eight o'clock a gay and gallant people was preparing on a sunlit morning busily for its *jour de fête*. Forty-five seconds later of all that gaiety and courage there was nothing left. Not anything. Certain legends linger. They say that four days later, when the process of excavation was begun, there was found in the vault of the prison a negro criminal, the sole survivor. They say that in a waistcoat pocket a watch was found, its hands pointing to half-past nine, a watch that had recorded ninety useless minutes in a timeless tomb. And there are other stories. The stories of fishermen who set sail early in the morning to return for their *déjeuner* to find ruin there; of servants whom their mistresses had sent out of the town on messages; of officials and business men who left the town on the seventh or sixth of May for Fort de France. They are very like the war stories you will hear of men who returned after a five minutes' patrolling of a trench to find nothing left of their dug-out nor the people in it. They are probably exaggerated when they are not untrue. And yet it was these stories, more than even the sight of St. Pierre itself, that made that tragedy actual to me.

"We were," I was told, "twenty-four of us young people one Sunday on a picnic. We would have another picnic on the following Sunday, we decided. When that Sunday came there were only three of us alive."

A European cannot picture in terms of any tragedy that is likely to come to him what that tragedy meant for the survivors of Martinique. It did not mean simply the death of twenty-eight thousand people: the loss of property and possession, the curtain for many years upon the prosperity of the island. It meant the cutting of their lives in half more completely than would mean for me the destruction of every stone and every inhabitant in London. It meant the loss of half their friends, half their families, half their possessions, half their lives.

"I left St. Pierre on the seventh," a man told me. "I was to be married on the ninth. I had come into Fort de France, leaving my fiancée behind to make some last arrangements. I cannot express the excitement with which I woke on that morning of the eighth. I was twenty-four. She was three years younger. It was the first time that either of us had been in love. And that was the last whole day, I told myself, that I should ever spend alone. It was so lovely a morning, too. Bright and clear. And after one of the worst nights that there can have ever been. Thunder and lightning and unceasing rain. The sunlight was a happy omen. Never had I known, never shall I know, anything like the happiness with which I dressed and bathed and shaved that morning. And then, just as I was finishing my coffee, there came those two explosions. They were terrific. They shook the entire island. But I wasn't frightened, Why should I be? What was there to connect them with Pelée? I went on, as the rest of us did, with what we had to do.

"For a while that morning life went on in Fort de France in its ordinary way. But soon you had begun to notice a worried look on people's faces. The sky was dark; a thin dust in which pebbles were mingled was falling over the town. Rumour had started. There was no news coming through from St. Pierre. The telephone line had been cut suddenly in the middle of a message, at the instant of the two explosions. Since then there had been silence.

"You know how it is when a rumour starts in a small place. The most fantastic stories get about. A porteuse from Carbet had reported that a fisherman had seen flames behind St. Pierre, and no one asked themselves how ever a porteuse could have done the twenty-eight kilometres from Carbet in two hours.

"I tried not to feel frightened. It was absurd to be frightened. No one had been frightened in St. Pierre the afternoon before, when I had left it. Earlier they had been frightened, yes; when those cinders had been falling in the streets, when lightning was flickering about the crater's mouth; when the day was dark with clouds; when the sugar factory by the Rivière Blanche was being swept away by boiling mud. They had been frightened then. But the scientists had told them there was no need to be afraid. The Governor and his wife had come out there themselves. The cinders had practically stopped falling. It was only old Pelée amusing himself again.

"That was what I told myself. But you know how it is when panic catches hold of a place. By eleven o'clock our nerves had gone. Three hours and still no news, with the wildest rumours flying round, not one of us could work.

We sat in the club, forgetting our rum punches, one thought only in our minds. I shall never forget that morning: the suspense, the terror, the uncertainty. Midday and still no message had come through. The boat that had been sent out to make enquiries had not returned. We sat and waited. It was not till one o'clock that we knew."

He paused and shrugged his shoulders.

"It's twenty-six years ago," he said. "That's a long time. One can forget most things in that time. One thinks one's heart broken. But it mends. One thinks one's life is over. But it isn't. One goes on living. One makes the best out of what's left. I've not had a bad best, either. I've had a happy marriage. I'm proud of my children. I've made a position. But," he again shrugged his shoulders, "I don't know that since that day I've felt that anything mattered in particular."

I think that in that anecdote is expressed what life has been for the whole of Martinique, for the whole of his generation of Martinique. The carrying on with life in face of the feeling that nothing really matters.

"GONE NATIVE"

IV

IN Tahiti, where American and English mails arrived simultaneously once a month, mail day invariably found one waiting outside the post office. In Martinique, where mails arrived at frequent and irregular intervals, one left the shipping office to forward one's letters as they came. I had no idea even that a boat was in when Armantine appeared one morning, carrying an envelope, across which trailed at varying angles Inez Holden's incredible calligraphy.

"As you know" (it ran), "I never begin or end my letters or answer other people's, though sometimes I just write. 'What is it like in the West Indies and are the natives nice?' This is a true quotation of a remark I heard fall from the lips of a débutante during dinner the other evening. Her hostess having put her next to a young man from 'foreign parts.' Actually I have no idea what your life can be like. The tropics to the ungeographical are, of course, as much of a mystery as the whole of modern life must always be to the unscientific. I might imagine you as having 'gone native' to the tune of barbaric tom-toms, fuzzy hair and prancing niggers, degraded to 'white cargo,' or whatever it is. However, I am quite open-minded and for all I know it may be much worse still, for you may be doing your best to be a 'white man' to the last, clinging to conventions and dressing for dinner stuffed in a stiff shirt every evening in your tropical 'oubliette.'

"Of London and your friends what have I to tell you? I am a very bad medium for news and have become more misanthropic than ever. The other morning the fog lifted and I walked in the park, where I encountered Harold Acton. He was altogether witty and enchanting from every aspect, but so like my imitation of him which once amused you, that it seemed as if my own words were echoing back to me."

It was a longish letter; there was talk of London, of our friends there; of her first novel, *Sweet Charlatan,* that was in the press.

"I am filled with horror at the idea," she wrote, "with all the swooning affectations of an actress at her first night, except that mine is not only affectation. Did you feel like this about your first novel? or were you too young to feel self-conscious? or is it so long ago that you've forgotten? And do you really like *Sweet Charlatan* as much as you said you did? Write and encourage me. Write, even if you can't encourage me. It would amuse me to read of your vast life in the tropics through the diminutive medium of your neat handwriting."

It was the first news that I had had from England for many days. London had begun to seem a very great way off. With a direct vividness that letter brought it back to me. Just as clearly as I could see Inez herself, loitering into Boulestin's in a scarlet coat held round by a black belt, a little carelessly worn, or hurrying back to her flat from a day's flying at the aerodrome, or laughing across a dinner table under the light of candles; just as clearly as I saw her could I see the world she wrote of: its parties and its personalities, its sights and sounds, its many-coloured stir of contacts. It was clear because it spoke of what was familiar. Language is a form of algebra. There must be a comprehended reality at the back of symbol. But what would that letter have conveyed to one who had never left Waikiki? And wondering that, I wondered whether these pages I was writing would convey any clear impression to the untravelled English and American.

For the tropics are completely different from anything that one expects. Out of plays and films and novels, out of the conversation of our friends we build a picture of what life is like between Aden and Sourabaya. We go there and it is not like that at all. When I first sailed for them I had a mental picture very much like that of Inez Holden. On the one hand there was the white man with his dinner jacket and his stiff shirt; on the other the "gone native" cabin, the emptying bottle of rum, the tumbling half-castes. I pictured the tropics as one place, in the same way that politically one talks of America and Germany as though one were speaking of a single person. I thought of the natives as white people with brown faces. The reality was completely different.

Certain aspects of that reality it is impossible to convey. Climate, which is a series of physical sensations, can scarcely be made real to any one who is virgin to those sensations. You cannot explain what snow is to a Marque-

129

san. Nor can you picture equatorial heat in terms of English heat. A heat which is just as trying, but of a different texture. Nor can the qualities of landscape be conveyed with any exactness. You can do little more than evoke in the reader's mind a conventional image of tropic scenery. No one, for instance, who has not been both to Malaya and Polynesia could appreciate the skill with which Somerset Maugham has differentiated their separate landscapes. Much there is that cannot be conveyed. But the disparity between what one expected and what one finds largely lies in the fact that the reality would have surprised one less if one had not expected anything at all.

Novels are a bad guide. Or rather, the novelist who has written of the tropics has been misread. Perhaps because he has dabbled in sociology so much, the novelist would appear to be regarded nowadays as the producer of unofficial blue-books. "This isn't a true picture," people will say. "How many people lead that kind of life? To how many people does that kind of experience come?" The novelist is adjured at the same time to tell stories and to portray the ordinary everyday life of ordinary people. If he describes a married woman in Penang arranging an illicit week in Singapore, he will be met with the criticism "That's not true of Penang. How many women have done that, d'you think?" Which is sociological but not literary criticism. He is expected to draw studies of society from which principles may be deduced. He is expected not only to entertain, but to fulfil a function. It is by this standard that the majority of novels seem to be reviewed. You might as well say to Edgar Wallace, "What percentage of people do you think are crooks?" It does not matter in the least whether any woman from Penang has or has not gone to Singapore to meet a lover; all that the novelist has to do is to make the reader believe that the particular woman he is describing in the particular story did. You cannot make a story out of the ordinary lives of ordinary people. Stories are made out of exceptional people, in ordinary circumstances, or ordinary people in exceptional circumstances. The background of ordinary life must be accurate; that is the only restriction that is laid upon the novelist. Because, however, the idea of the tropics is so strange to the Western mind, the exceptional character and circumstances that the novelist has described are accepted as being general.

In one of his best stories, *The Outstation*, Somerset Maugham has portrayed a district officer in Borneo leading, a week's journey from the nearest town, the same life that he would have lived in his club in Pall Mall. Every evening he wore a stiff white shirt, and patent leather shoes. It is true. Everything that can be put across is true. You know that that particular man in that situation would behave in that way. He is, however, exceptional. I have not yet met a man who wore evening clothes in the tropics in the bush. In the towns one wears evening clothes as one would in London, a white coat taking the place of the dinner jacket. On the plantations one wears what is most comfortable. Usually one wears the native dress: a sarong, or Chinese trousers. The stiff white shirt character is as rare as the "gone native" character. For him, too, I have never met. I have heard stories of men recognising in native kampongs among troupes of itinerant musicians the features of men they were at school with. But such stories have always reminded me of those anecdotes with whose example at school one's house-master used to exhort one to good behaviour. Anecdotes of the shabby, drink-sodden creature coming to beg for half-a-crown. "In the whole of his lying story the one thing I could verify was the fact that once he had been captain of this school." In the tropics, as elsewhere, people have gone to pieces. But the man who would go to pieces in the tropics would go to pieces anywhere. And in the popular imagination the "gone native" myth has become identified with that very different, very real problem of the tropics—the white man and the brown woman.

§

How considerable a problem it is only those, I think, who have lived in the tropics can appreciate. The situation amounts to this: that a man during his first ten years in the tropics can scarcely afford to marry, and that for the unmarried man there is no practical alternative between chastity and the brown woman. The white man outnumbers the white woman by fifteen to one. The white women that are there, are, for the most part, the wives of residents. There are no unattached or unchaperoned young women. Occasionally there are scandals. But if only for lack of opportunities they are rare. Privacy is difficult in a community not only where every one knows everybody, and what every one is doing at any given moment, but in which there are neither locked doors nor doors to lock, where every verandah is open to casual scrutiny. There is no semi-underworld. Occasionally the town will be visited by a troupe of singers. Occasionally a French saleswoman will arrive with Paris fashions. But that is all; for the most part the white life of a tropical town is consequently extremely moral.

In French colonies the situation presents no difficulties. The French have little colour feeling. Their Empire is a black one. They have, moreover, the mistress system. They expect a young man to have his *"petite amie,"* till the time for a prudent marriage comes. The British Empire, however, is white. And its young men are officially expected to remain chaste until they marry. Whatever is done by the Englishman has to be done secretly. And it is idle to pretend that vice in the East is anything but a very squalid business. Orientals, even when they love, are matter-of-fact. Over vice they throw no glamour. It would be impossible to throw any over the whispered message to a head boy on a lonely evening, the impatient pacing of a dark verandah; the silent tread of a half-seen dusky figure; the attempt to create a companionable atmosphere with a gramophone and cakes and *stengahs;* the hurrying back before dawn to the waiting rickshaw. That ordinarily is what it is. Sometimes the experiment of a second establishment is made, and a man is told, jocularly, that he speaks Malay too well, but it is furtive and unsatisfactory. It is impossible to visit the establishment very often. It is expensive. The white man suspects with good reason that he is being deceived by all his servants. As often as not the experiment is abandoned. There is no sense of liberty, no sense of companionship.

"The trouble is," a young business man in Penang said

to me, "that there's no place where you can get friendly with the girls. One would thank heaven here for the kind of night club like the '67 that in London one wouldn't put one's nose inside." To the young bachelor that side of life cannot be anything but profoundly unsatisfying. Any averagely attractive white girl arriving in the tropics will be deluged with proposals of marriage.

In the plantations and in towns that are not British possessions the situation is slightly different. In Bangkok, for example, it would be possible for a white man to have a Siamese girl living in his bungalow, and on the plantations there is fairly often a Malay girl who disappears discreetly when visitors arrive. There the relationship has a certain dignity. There is faithfulness on both side. Custom creates affection. But in neither case is there any approach to the "gone native" picture. In neither case has the white man done anything that involves loss of caste. He observes the customs of the country. To the average Westerner, of course, the idea of a white person living with a brown is intensely revolting. But the average Westerner thinks of the coloured races in terms of negroes.

I was discussing Robert Keable's novel, *Numerous Treasure*, with a woman who had lived a great deal of her life in the Antilles.

"It's good enough," she said. "But when you think of what it amounts to really: a white man living with the kind of girl you see about the villages."

"But that's not the type of girl at all," I said, "that Keable's writing about. He's not writing about niggers. He's writing about Polynesians."

"I suppose they are a bit different, really," she admitted.

The Eskimo and the Hindoo are not more different. The Laos, the Malays, the Polynesians are proud, free-born people with a culture and traditions. They are completely separate from one another. But they have in common a heritage of personal dignity. They cannot be spoken of as the South African negro or the Australian aborigines.

All the same, I believe it is extremely rare for there to exist a profound relationship between a white man and a brown woman. The Polynesian, sweet-natured and tender though she is, is in too simple a state of development to attach permanently to herself a modern Westerner. While though the Malays and Siamese have an old and complicated culture, it is invariably with Malays and Siamese of the coolie class that the white man allies himself and under conditions which preclude romance. These relationships, into whatever they may develop, begin as a business transaction with the parents of the girl. There is no process of selection. It is arranged through the head boy. You might just as hopefully expect a profound experience to come from the answering of an advertisement in *Le Sourire*.

In most novels of the East, written by men who know the East, no attempt is made to disguise this fact. "The exceptional circumstance" that is introduced to make the story interesting is spontaneous feeling on the girl's part. Usually it is the story, as in *Spears of Deliverance* and *Sepia*, of a man who resists the ordinary situation to yield ultimately to a girl's wooing. These novels do not attempt to pretend that this situation is anything but exceptional. Novels are written out of dreams. It is in this way that the white man in the East dreams of things happening. They rarely do. Ninety-nine times in a hundred there is the discussion with a head boy, the bargaining with a parent. There is no glamour. There is no selection. "It's a bit difficult at first," I was told. "You've nothing to talk to her about except the price of paddy. After a while, you come to have things in common. You get pretty fond of her."

It was a teak man in North Siam who said that to me. "We can't take them up into the jungle with us," he went on. "We're there for ten months of the year. Perhaps that's why we're so faithful to them. They don't have a chance of getting on our nerves."

It is very much in that spirit that the majority of white men in the far East regard these establishments. In Europe such relationships are exercising at the moment a powerful appeal on the popular imagination. The number of novels dealing with the subject is a proof of that. It is an expression, that interest, of the desire to get a thing both ways. The European imagines that in such a situation he will know the excitement of illicit love and the comforts of domesticity. But it is not like that. He is free. He has domesticity. But love he has not got. I have yet to meet the man who will say that he has really loved a coloured woman. In the work of no writer except Kipling—and women are a side-show in Kipling's mental make-up; in many of his greatest stories women do not appear at all— is there any attempt to pretend that love as the moderns know it can exist under such conditions. Only twice does Somerset Maugham make a relationship with a coloured woman binding upon a white. And in each case he chose a Chinese woman. Love, as we understand it, is foreign to these people.

"Son desire tout sensuel," wrote Maupassant—he was speaking of the Arabs—"n'est point de ceux qui dans nos pays à nous montraient aux ètoilles par des nuits pareilles. Sur cette terre amollissante et tiède, si captivante que la légende des Lotophages y est né dans l'ile de Djerba, l'air est plus savoureux que partout, le soleil plus chaud, le jour plus clair. Mais le cœur ne sait pas aimer, les femmes belles et ardentes sont ignorante de nos tendresses. Leurs ames simples reste étrangères aux emotions sentimentales et leurs baisers, dit-on, n'enfantent point le reve."

Tahiti has been called the country of love, but Western love does not exist there. The Tahitians set no store by the things we value highest. "I suppose," I once heard it asked, "that the Tahitians make love as readily as a modern girl will kiss?" But the answer is, "Much more readily." The kiss is to the Tahitian a proof of affection. She will kiss no one of whom she is not fairly fond. Love-making she regards as a kind of dance. An adequate partner is all she needs. She regards that partner as the English girl regards a dancing partner. You do not kiss every man you dance with. The Tahitian who is ready to make love with a complete stranger might be offended if that stranger spoke of love to her. To an American, who was leaving for San Francisco for a couple of months, his Tahitian mistress said on their last evening, "Whatever you do, don't kiss any other girl."

Tahiti is love's land. Love there is freely given. There are no discussions with head boys; no bargaining with parents; there are no responsibilities. No girl will be reluctant to have children in a country where children are well loved, where life is easy and life is happy. For the believer in free love Tahiti will seem the realisation of all his dreams. And I am not sure that Tahiti's lesson to the white man is not the discovery that there is no such thing as free love; that where love is free there is no love; that he neither loves nor is loved who has no bonds laid on him; that it is not the person who gives to you, but the person to whom you give who matters; that to the person to whom you have given something of yourself you are bound permanently, since you must return to that person if you would be complete; which is a thing that the person who has divided himself between many loves can never be. The Don Juans declare that they are searching for the ideal mate. They are not. They are searching for themselves; they are unsatisfied because they are incomplete. It is not vaingloriousness but the desire that her whole life and being shall be in the hands of a new lover that drives women to those confessions that cost her in the end that new lover's faith in her.

Tahiti is love's land. It warms and softens; it lays the heart bare in readiness to love. But I have not met a single white man who has found love there with a Tahitian. "Leurs baisers n'enfantent point le reve."

Between brown and white there can be only a brief and superficial harmony. Such is the universal experience and the universal testimony of those in a position to judge accurately. Between brown and white there can be no relation interesting in itself. The interest lies in the situations that such relationships create. There are the half-caste children that have to be educated; there is the problem of the white wife who may come to a district in which her husband, as a bachelor, has had a coloured mistress; there is the wrench of leaving the brown woman when it is all over. Those situations are interesting. But the actual relationship I do not believe has ever gone very deep. And the greatest surprise to the traveller in the tropics will be to find how very little store is placed upon that side of life. In Siam, particularly, I noted this.

SIAM

V

My visit to Siam was an unprepared adventure. They talk of the unhurrying East. And that, of course, it is. In a climate where a two-minute stroll reduces you to a state of damp prostration, life must move slowly if it is to be endured. But that is not to say that it is unadventurous. On the contrary, the very fact that it is unhurrying increases its potentiality for surprise. As for example:

It was in Penang, at the hour of ginsling, which is not the Malayan equivalent for cocktail time, but the morning break at the hour when people begin to weary of their offices. Between a quarter and half-past eleven there is a drifting towards those rival Harrod's, Pritchard's, and John Little's for twenty minutes of restoring gossip. It was in Pritchard's at the hour of the ginsling. And we were discussing, some four or five of us, Reginald Campbell's *Uneasy Virtue*, a novel that had its setting half in

143

Penang and half in the teak jungles of North Siam. "I wonder," I said, "how far it really is like that?" Adding in the idle way one does, "It would be rather fun to go and see."

It was the kind of remark that in England would have been countered with a vague "Ah, yes." Or a discussion preferred, ironically, on the limitations and brevity of life. But in the East, whence half the fairy stories of the world have come, where magic carpets and bottled genii are no more than exaggerations of a way of living, there is the danger always of being taken at your word. "Then why," said one of the party, "don't you go there?"

In a moment I had embarked on such a series of excuses as the cautious and calculating habits of Western life forge for us. But it was too late. The words of the spell were uttered. The genie was wreathing into smoke out of the bottle's neck. The edges of the carpet had begun to lift. "That should be quite simple," my friend was saying. "Let me see, now. There's a man I know, a forest officer, who's going to make a jungle tour next week. He's starting for the north on Sunday. It's Wednesday now. If you left here on Friday morning you'ld be in Bangkok before dark on Saturday; that just fits. We'll wire and see if he can take you." Before I had realised what was happening a telegraph form had been requisitioned and the genie had begun his work.

That is the way things happen in the East. In Europe we make plans months ahead and we adhere to them. In the heat of summer we book our rooms in Switzerland for winter sports. Every seat on the Blue train is sold while the croisette is a succession of shuttered windows. Like

144

the billiard player, we think three strokes ahead. In January we make our plans for June. Life moves so quickly that we should be submerged otherwise. But in the countries that are south of Aden no man bothers overmuch about what he will be doing a fortnight hence. Plans mature swiftly in that country of easy growth. Suggestions are made casually. "Wouldn't it be rather fun?" says some one. And you agree eagerly. Nor, on the next morning, do you write one of those notes so eminently practical with their justifying quotation from Mrs. Browning to the effect that "colours seen by candlelight do not look the same by day," to explain how, on thinking it over in cool blood, you really feel . . .

A jungle trip is not a thing that can be undertaken lightly. It requires very careful adjustments of commissariat. You have to carry your larder with you. It is not pleasant to find yourself without provisions a hundred miles from any road that can be described as "Fordable." But the days pass so slowly that the ordering of six elephants instead of four and thirty-five coolies instead of twenty is an unalarming enterprise. There is always time to remedy mistakes. Things wait for you to catch them up.

Eighty-six hours later I was in Bangkok.

§

Bangkok is a surprising city.

It is advertised as the Venice of the East. It photographs exquisitely. There are its proud avenues; the stately proportion of the throne hall; the strangely shaped and strangely coloured temples; its dark, mysterious canals. But the prevailing impression that it leaves on you is of dust and heat and squalor. The temples and the palaces are far apart. They are divided from one another by hot white roads and sequences of ugly buildings. The avenues are lined by insignificant and unsightly cabins. The city was planned by an earlier monarch who did not realise that Siam was without enough rich people to adorn fittingly those avenues with spacious bungalows. And as you drive past shack after wooden shack you wonder whether the temple and avenues and palaces are anything more than a façade, imposing and distorting, before the real Siam that has expressed itself in the wooden and tin huts that crowd the canal and streets, and in the sluggish barges that float down its sluggish waterways. Siam is trying to Westernise itself. And, paradoxically, it is at the same time plying the slogan of "Siam for the Siamese." The new *régime* is removing all the Europeans that it can from official positions, and those it is forced to retain are treated so cavalierly that many of them have presented their resignations. But the real Siam, the wealth and spirit of Siam, is apart from and indifferent to those changes. You suspect this while you are still in Bangkok. You are convinced of it within an hour of your leaving: as the train rattles through a landscape that has been, and for its geographical position must remain, exclusively agricultural.

§

Chiengmai, the northern capital, is twenty-seven hours of railroad north of Bangkok. In the old days, when there was no railway, you had to go by water. It was a five weeks' journey. The construction of the railway has brought vast differences into the life of those northern states, so separate from the southern states—they are more in touch with Burma than Siam—that they speak different languages and employ in places a different currency. But even so Chiengmai is a very distant city. It is the timber trade that brings the white man to Siam, and Chiengmai is the administrative centre of the two chief companies, the Borneo and the Bombay Burma. There are not, I fancy, more than thirty white people in the station. There is the bank manager and the English consul; there are the forest manager, and an occasional assistant who has come in from the jungle for a rest; there is an American mission which is responsible for schools and hospitals and a big sanatorium for lepers. The white life of Chiengmai centres round the Gymkhana Club. It is a large field set a little way out of town which serves as polo ground and golf course and tennis court. By five o'clock, when the heat of the day has lessened, most of the white community is there, scattered about the field. There is seventy-five minutes of strenuous exercise. Then when the light fails there is a gathering round a large table on which have been set out drinks, glasses and a little lamp. There are rarely more and rarely less than a dozen people there. It is peaceful. In the swift-fallen dusk the large field, with its wide-branched trees rising from a hedge, looks heart-breakingly like an English meadow. Mosquitoes are buzz-ing round the table. The women have slipped their legs into sarongs, sewn up at one end in the shape of bags. The talk is subdued and intimate. It is the hour that makes amends for the heat and dust of morning and afternoon. But it is not easy to convey the essence of those evenings. "What," I can hear the protest of the average townsman, "you call this the best hour of the day; sitting round a table talking to people you've seen every evening of the week for as many years as you may happen to have been there? And the only variety, you say, is when one of the assistants, a fellow about whom you know all that there is to know, comes in for a few days from the jungle, or one of the men from Bangkok, about whom you know everything that there is to know, comes up for a jungle trip.

"And the only festivity, you say, is the Christmas meet, when the assistants come in from the jungle. But that would only mean about fifty people all told. And, anyhow, they would be people that you know already. My word, I can't imagine anything more terrible. I should think that they'ld all be on each other's nerves so completely that they'ld be wanting to cut each other's throats."

If you were to picture Chiengmai in terms of England that is what it would be like and that is what would happen. But you cannot picture it in terms of England. Chiengmai is so far and the whites there are so few. Their life is hard and testing. It has many dangers, many difficulties. It is only by mutual tolerance, by interdependence, by loyalty and friendship that it can be made tolerable. In most small communities you will find gossiping and malice and petty spite. But in Chiengmai you will not. The white community has the solidarity of a small band united against a common foe.

§

During the month that I spent in the jungle I was to realise the nature and capacities of that foe. We were three of us who made the trip. The Siamese Government leaves to certain companies the right to work for a number of years certain sections of forest land. There are a number of restrictions laid upon the companies, and the two men with whom I was travelling were making a tour of inspection on behalf of the Government to see that the agreements were being faithfully carried out.

During the war I often felt that life in a quiet part of the line would be rather a pleasant picnic if one were without responsibilities; if one had not to inspect the packing of limbers and the equipment of one's men; if the moment one arrived, hot and weary after a long march, one could rest in one's dug-out instead of having to rush round gun emplacements to see that one's men were settled in. In Siam that wish was granted. It was the war without its danger and without its responsibilities. We travelled with an establishment of nine elephants and forty coolies. The hard work of camping was taken off our shoulders. At quarter to six in the morning we woke to a cup of tea and the sound of packing. While we dressed and breakfasted at our leisure the camp was struck. Our bedding and our food were stacked on elephants and coolies' shoulders. The supervision was in the hands of a head boy. By half-past seven our ponies were waiting for us and our procession was half an hour's march away. Elephants move slowly. Two miles an hour is the maximum. Fourteen miles is a long day's march. Not that you can picture jungle miles in terms of English miles. Along the majority of the roads you could not drag a

bullock cart. For the most part you are piloting yourself
with the aid of a heavy staff along steep and stony paths
or slithering over slippery paddy fields. The streams
through which you wade are high above your knees. The
average village road is a narrow isthmus of caked mud
running between bogs into which you are likely to slide
every seven steps. You are caked in mud. You are soaked
with sweat. The mornings are few during the autumn
when you are not drenched with a heavy downpour of
rain. You are very weary by the time you reach, after a
seven-hour march, the compound on the stream by which
you are to spend the night. You sit forward on a log,
limp and motionless, while the coolies cut away a clearing
in the bush and your boys run up your tent and your cook
prepares your tiffin. You are too tired to talk over your
meal, and the moment it is over you fling yourself upon
your bed. In a couple of minutes you are asleep.

§

The country through which you travel is varied.

The word "jungle" evokes a picture of tangled undergrowth, of scarlet macaws, of monkeys screaming to each
other from every bough, of large many-coloured butterflies, of snakes and bears and natives shooting at you from
behind hills with blowpipes. It may be that in South
America that is what it is. But in Siam it is a friendly
landscape. There are cobra, it is true, but you rarely
meet them. I only saw a couple of small snakes, neither
of which was poisonous probably. You will hear the
screech of monkeys, but they remain invisible. Though

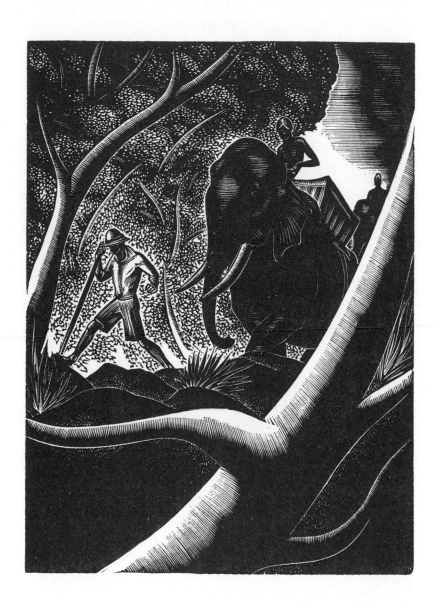

you will come upon the tracks of a bear, the bear is an animal that must be hunted. And though the foliage is in places overpoweringly luxuriant, the country is for the most part open. The flat land is planted with rice, and the undergrowth is inconsiderable in the actual forests.

The Laos are quiet, simple, decently-lived people. They cultivate their rice, carry their produce to the markets, tend their animals and chew their betel nut. And though, when you ask how far it is to such a place, you will be answered in such simple methods of reckoning as "Half a bullock's march" or "As far as you can hear a dog bark," it is hard to believe that you are a hundred miles from a road, from what is called civilisation. It is only at odd moments that you will realise how remote these people are from the practical organisation of the big cities.

When, for example, you purchase a six-satang object with a tical, you will receive as your change not the ninety-four satangs you expect, but eighty or eighty-one. You count the change over three times. Then protest. The shopkeeper shakes his head. "We are giving eighty-five satangs for a tical."

"But the tical," you say, "is worth a hundred satangs."

"Oh, no, at the most not more than eighty-seven."

For a while, perhaps, you will argue. Then you will decide that thirteen-hundredths of one and tenpence are not worth quarrelling over. You will seek enlightenment. "It's quite simple," it will be explained to you. "The tical is too big a coin for these people. It's a nuisance to them and they can't get rid of it easily. They say it isn't worth more than eighty-five satangs to them. It's rather like a man in a remote English village saying that it'll be a

153

fearful nuisance to him changing a five-pound note. None of his friends will be able to. He won't be able to buy anything with it. He'll have to wait for a chance of changing it. But that if you care to take ninety shillings for it you can have it.

"At one time," he will go on, "we used to have all the men's wages sent up here in copper coins by donkeys. But it didn't pay, we found. It was more trouble than it was worth. In fact, you're really lucky to get as much as eighty-five satangs for a shilling."

It is at such moments that you realise how distant from civilisation the Lao still is, but for the most part you feel that you are in as ordered and developed a world as you would in Europe within half an hour's stroll of telephones and cars. Their villages are tidy, their huts clean and airy, their single store is bright with printed cotton. Each village has its temple and its school. And the presence of the priests, with their cropped heads and their yellow robes, lend a dignity to life. The complicated Buddhist faith, over which metaphysicians will split hairs indefinitely, is a direct and simple thing to the simple Laos. They have retained the capacity to wonder.

§

A few weeks before my arrival a white elephant, the sacred symbol of the faith, the occasion years back of war with Burma, had been born on one of the teak company's workings. Such a thing had not happened within the memory of man. For miles round the villagers came to pay it homage. Every evening, when the calf was brought down to the river to be bathed, a hundred and fifty to two hundred people were gathered in the compound. They wore their richest and brightest clothes. They had brought flowers to cast before the infant's feet. And sugar cane to refresh the mother. There was a hush of religious awe. The brown eyes of the Lao maidens grew wide and solemn, luminous and dilated. Their lips parted in a sigh. Their little crinkled hands were joined together, lifted before their faces in simple and silent worship as the calf trotted turbulently towards the water.

It was a curious and moving sight, and I could not help following the curving sequence of analogy as I watched the pink urchin bound and leap in the brown water. There it sported, like genius in a nursery, unaware that there was any difference between its playmates and itself, unconscious of its own importance, undreaming of its fate and future, the high rewards, the applause, the honour. All along the analogy held. Like genius it had won tardily to recognition.

The rider who presented himself with the news that his charge had given birth to a white elephant was laughed at. There was a sad smile on the district assistant's face as he started his interrogation. To begin with, he asked, how many toes had it? Eighteen, he was told, and, that, in his view, settled it. All real white elephants had twenty. But the rider was persistent. The elephant was no ordinary one. Would not the *nai* be gracious enough to come and see it? In the end the assistant went. It was the waste of a day, but one had to humour a good rider. When he saw it, however, the pitying smile changed to one of wonder. He had never seen a white elephant in infancy. There are not so very many people in the world who have. But the pink urchin that tottered between its mother's legs was emphatically unlike any calf that he had seen before.

The report he sent into Chiengmai was the occasion for loud and continued laughter. It was suggested that he should try the wagon. But the weeks passed, and the calf, instead of growing darker, became each day more faintly pink. All along the analogy held good—the mistrust of relatives, the incredulous contempt of critics, the admittance made grudgingly at last that "at least there was something unusual here," their refusal definitely to commit themselves. For the critics are never happy till they have qualified their testimonial, till they have contrived a loophole for their escape should their swan reveal itself to be a goose. The experts remained dubious about those eighteen toes.

The Laos themselves, who are the public, had no doubt, however. The calf's progress to Chiengmai was regal. And later, when vindication came, in the same way that genius when it visits poverty will lift out of obscurity a host of humble people, so did this freak of birth bring recompense to the associates of its infancy. Not alone was it to march to triumph. For the director of the teak company there was royalty's recognition. For the rider— that ignorant Lao peasant—there was at Bangkok in the royal stables the dignity of leisured comfort. For the mother, that blind fulfiller of destiny, there had come an end for ever to the harsh jungle days. She was never to know work. Ended her days of *ounging* and *tontawing;* the long, heavily burdened marches under a tropic sun; the dragging of timber, the breaking up of stacks. She was immune. She had mothered prodigy. She was entitled to an old age of honoured ease. All along the analogy held good. And there was a quality curiously satisfying in the thought that somewhere in the jungle still, unhonoured and unrecognised, the anonymous begetter of divinity, the chance partner in a haphazard coupling, was trumpeting his servitude to "the reverberate hills."

§

We were inspecting the workings of the Borneo and of the Bombay Burma companies. And most of the time was spent with one or other of the assistants.

The work of an assistant consists mainly in long marches to supervise the work in the various sections of his district. There is a good deal to supervise. First of all there is the selection and girdling of the trees that are to be felled. Girdling is the process by which the sap is prevented from rising, so that the tree is dry and floatable when the time comes later for it to be felled. The logs are then dragged by elephants to the river. It takes four or five years for a log to float to Bangkok. Very often there are blocks along the way. During the dry season at the river's bends the logs will heap themselves into immense stacks which have to be broken up by elephants. There are also to be arranged the innumerable details of road-making and commissariat. The district is large that each assistant covers. He has a big central compound where he keeps his clothes and books. But the greater part of the time he is on the march. Sometimes he has a rest house to stay in. As often as not he clears himself a camp near a stream where his elephants can water.

The weeks we spent there were very like a picnic. But I could picture what the life of the assistant must be during ordinary periods. For months on end, through the sequence of rain-drenched weeks, he might never see a white man. There would be no cheery companionship at the end of a long day's marching; no antidote to the maladies of jungle life, the discomfort; the itch of prickly heat, the leeches, the mosquitoes and the mud-sores; the sandflies that no netting can keep out; the red ants that night after night make sleep impossible; the long depression of the September rains, when bedding and kit are soaked and for days it is impossible to wear dry clothing; the fever that takes its toll, slowly, spasm by spasm, of your vitality and courage. Fever comes suddenly upon you, and in a few hours you are incapable of movement. I remember returning to a compound where three hours earlier we had said "Good-bye" to a strong and vigorous assistant, to find waiting for us a pale, lined, white-faced figure laid out on a long chair, shivering with a rug over him. I could not believe that it was the same man.

It is in a place such as Northern Siam that the question of the brown woman is insistent. Siam is a hard country for the white woman. In the earlier days assistants were not encouraged to marry. And though the construction of the railway has brought Chiengmai into close touch with the basis of civilisation, and though the greater capacities of the modern girl has made it possible for a man to run the risk of bringing a white wife with him, the girls are not many with the courage and strength to face the loneliness and monotony of station life. It depends on the type of girl that one attracts and is attracted by. As one man said to me: "The only type of woman that I'ld care to marry would go mad in five weeks in a place like this."

For such a one the alternative of the brown woman is difficult to avoid. It is not so much actual physical necesity as the need, when one returns to Chiengmai, to find waiting there a friendly and familiar atmosphere. During the war the one thing that the soldier longed for was a quiet domestic life; an ordered routine, with a train to be caught each morning and slippers warmed against his return. In the same way the young assistant, seated at nightfall on his verandah, will picture to himself a house well kept and comfortable and affection waiting him.

It is an issue to which no moral principles are attached. There is no loss of caste. It is a matter of the practical management of one's life. To a Lao the mere fact of living together constitutes marriage. Such relationships are decently and honourably lived. The children are well educated. Very often when children are born the white man marries. At any rate he leaves his consort properly provided for when he returns to Europe. The question for him to decide is whether by such an arrangement life is going to be made simpler and happier for him. He knows what he is in for. He makes his choice open-eyed. Some decide one way, some another. It is, I should say, the minority of the younger men nowadays who enter into such arrangements.

But, either way, it is not a problem that bulks largely in the white man's eyes. He acquires something of the Oriental attitude to women. In Europe and America, where love in films and plays and novels is a highly advertised commodity, where 90 per cent. of the shops in a big city are designed to attract women, life centres round women. In the Far East woman is a side-show.

That is the big surprise that awaits the woman who marries a man in the Far East.

§

At first she fancies she has come to a woman's paradise. From a position of probably no very great importance, from a small house and a life of many cares, she is transported to a large house, a dignified position, an ample and a leisured life. In England only a very few people can imagine themselves to be anything more than very small cogs in a very large machine, but in the East, by the mere fact of being white, you are a person of prominence.

The young bride who in her own home is no more than one of many, finds herself in Penang and Ipoh and Kuala Lumpur what is the equivalent of being a member of the aristocracy. She is definitely of the ruling class.

She has a large and wide-verandahed house. She has a large staff of servants over whom she has complete control. She does not live, as her mother does, in terror of her cook and maids. She can discharge an entire staff at breakfast in the certainty of being able to replace it in time for tiffin. She has to do practically no work. She gives the vaguest of orders in the morning knowing that if she brings four people back to dinner after a *pahit* party her Malay cook will provide a meal for them at a moment's notice with equanimity.

No Malay cook is ever unprepared. He works in collaboration with his friends. He enjoys what amounts to the amenities of a communal kitchen. He knows what parties are going on at what bungalows. He knows from whom he can borrow some soup, from whom some fish, from whom a savoury. He regards your crockery and silver along with those of your friends as destined for general use. It is by no means unusual to go out to dinner and find your own fish knives and forks set in front of you. All of which makes the business of housekeeping extremely simple.

A white woman in the East, even if she has a large family, has really very little to do except amuse herself, and there are countless opportunities for that.

With the men outnumbering the women by ten to one, she is surrounded with invitations to dance, to play tennis, to golf, to motor and to swim. She need never be lonely for want of *beaux*, nor are there any competing attractions. In no other part of the world does a woman find herself so completely without rivals. In England a woman's men friends lead a private and personal life, which she herself scarcely ever sees. In Malaya there is no such life.

She is the only type of woman a man can meet otherwise than secretly. She has a monopoly that makes her superficially as powerful as is the American woman in the States—only superficially, however, for whereas the American woman not only looks but is important, governing and directing public opinion through her clubs, in the Far East the white woman counts for very little.

The East is a man's world. A world of pioneers, of men who have abandoned their homes in a spirit of adventure to develop a strange country, and the pioneer is occupied pretty exclusively with his own job. He is there to produce rubber, to sell copra, to dredge for tin. His work is his life.

In London, a very large percentage of masculine conversation deals with women; in the East you will hear them very little mentioned, even by the younger men. The conversation there is concerned with sport, with shares, with questions of policy and administration. Woman is a side-show.

One thinks always of the tropics in terms of glamour and romance. One has seen so many films, one has read so many descriptions of moonlit nights and palm trees, of golden sands, and softly lapping waters. But Malaya is not Polynesia. Penang is as lovely as Tahiti, but no two islands could be more different. Which is the reason, I think, why women weary of the East; why those first eager letters give way to prosaic bulletins of facts that are succeeded in their turn, as often as not, by indifference and discontent; why they are so ready, when the time comes, to accompany their children to Europe instead of remaining with their husbands.

The East is foreign to them—foreign and unwelcoming. They feel that it has cheated them. It has not given them the richness that it had seemed to offer. It has its glamour. But it is not the glamour they expected. In Europe and in America one thinks of glamour and romance

in terms of women, but in the East romance is represented by the very real fortitude, patience and strength
of those who have developed, in a hundred years, a strange
and hostile country into a happy and prosperous de-
pendency.

CEYLON

VI

IT is as well to leave a place when leaving it can still make you a little sad, and as Eldred Curwen and I rowed away from Martinique at half-past two on a cloudless morning towards the *Nova Scotia* we sincerely regretted the little bungalow at Case Navire. The moon was full; across the harbour we could hear the barbaric rhythms of the Bal Lou-Lou. Should we, we wondered, find anywhere else anything so lovely and so strange?

Quarter of an hour later we were wondering whether we had ever been to Martinique at all. We were on an English ship. The passages and the decks were clean, the metal of door handle and porthole shone. Stewards were arranging our luggage with the gruff amiability of sailors. In the saloon copies of *Harper's Bazaar* and *Nash's* were lying side by side. On the notice board a wireless message stated that at Melbourne the M.C.C. had made three hundred and seven for five wickets. Martinique, for all that its palm trees were outlined against the sky, seemed a century of miles away.

And next morning, after having been presented with a breakfast menu containing three and twenty items, we came on deck to see the white houses of Roseau spread along a hill-shadowed bay. It looked French, and, lying as it does midway between Martinique and Guadeloupe, with its background of French history and its natives still speaking Creole, it is in its sympathies more French than English. But when you stand at the head of the gangway, though the negro boatmen shout at you from the water, there is a smartly-dressed policeman at your side. "Which boat, sir, would you like?" he asks. You tell him. He calls out the name of the boat and the other boats stand back. When you reach the landing stage there is a policeman waiting so that there is no haggling about your fare. Though the feeling of the town is French, the streets are clean and the life is orderly. In the botanical gardens there is a cricket field. It was as complete a change of atmosphere as had been for me two years and a half back the stepping on to the decks of the *Kinta* at Singapore.

That was the most welcome change of atmosphere I have ever known. It came at the end of the worst month of travel I have ever known.

To begin with there was the Red Sea.

The Red Sea in the middle of August, when in addition to that monstrous heat there was a following breeze to still such poor current of air as the ship's slow movement brought. For four days the smoke rose perpendicularly to the blue-green sky. For four days I lay in a hammock chair wondering through hour after interminable hour whether the momentary rapture of iced beer compensated for the hour of intolerable discomfort that must ensue; while over-hot and over-tired infants who could not sleep and would not rest squabbled over their toys and fell about and bruised themselves and howled. Then with Djibouti passed, we met as we turned the corner of Gardafui the full fury of the monsoon. For six days under a lowering sky, through a grey and angry sea, the ship pitched and rolled and tossed its two thousand odd miles towards Ceylon. For six days I lay in a hammock chair, with hand and eyes half-closed, listening to the infants being sick, wondering whether the attempt to work up an appetite by a resolute patrolling of the deck would be certain to culminate in disaster. A ghastly voyage.

Before I was half-way across the Indian Ocean I had sworn that no power should keep me on the *Amboise* a day longer than was strictly necessary. I decided to break my journey at Colombo.

I regretted it. For every tourist there must be one place at which he will regret his stay; one place excellent in itself, at which expectation will be unrealised, at which for some reason or other everything will go wrong. Ceylon is that place for me. It was my own fault. I had not meant to break my journey there. I had made no preparation for staying. And Colombo is not a good place for the casually-presented stranger. In the nature of its geographical position that must be so. It is the most considerable port of call in the world. All the Australian traffic, all the Far East traffic, much of the Indian traffic passes through it. A great many ships spend a couple of days there. The streets and hotels are filled with tourists. In self-defence the resident population has built for itself an interior and self-contained society. The tourist, arriving with the average letter of introduction, is received in much the same way that such a one would be in Europe.

The man on whom I called was extremely affable.

"I am glad to see you," he said. "Let's see, now. I'm pretty full up this week. Tuesday, Wednesday, Thursday, Friday. What about Saturday, now? Let's lunch on Saturday."

He was a pleasant fellow, and I enjoyed our lunch. But I decided that I would not present any of the other letters I had brought with me. By the time I had decided that, the *Amboise* was well out to sea. It would be a week before the next Messageries boat arrived. "This," I thought, "is going to be a pretty difficult week to fill."

It was.

One letter that I had brought I did decide to present, however. It was addressed to Mr. Gimvo Sanjbo, and had been given me at the last moment before I left by the foreign representative of Shepherdson and Gray's oil, paint and enamel factory.

"Look here," he had said. "You had better see something of the native side of the place. This fellow must be one of the richest people there. He's the biggest buyer we've got between Cairo and Singapore. I'll tell him that you'll be turning up."

I went.

The rickshaw coolie, to whom I gave the address, looked puzzled for a moment, cogitated, then nodded his head. "I know," he said. "I take you."

With the resolute, steady swing of one who begins a
Marathon he set off along a broad well-paved street with
large buildings set back proudly from the roadway; after
a mile or so the street grew narrower and rougher. The
stature of the houses lessened. White faces became less
frequent. The pavement and the street were crowded. Another mile and the street became a road, the houses had
become shacks, from whose doorways scarlet-mouthed
Tamils spat betel juice upon the sidewalk. The noise was
deafening. Stories of kidnapped white men fretted my
memory like mosquitoes. I had seen a film that began
this way. A rickshaw hurrying down streets that every
yard grew narrower.

"Look here," I shouted. "In heaven's name, where are
you taking me?"

The coolie made no answer. His shoulders worked the
faster; just as they had in the film.

"Look here," I began.

Before I could finish the sentence, the rickshaw had
turned suddenly to the right, into a side street, narrower
than I could have conceived compatible with traffic, and
had drawn up suddenly before a long, low, one-storied
cabin above which on a weather-beaten board was painted
in faded lettering Gimvo Sanjbo. I stared at it with
amazement. I was assured now of the coolie's honesty.
He was no more than ignorant.

"No, no," I said, "this is not the place." And, taking
the letter from my pocket, I pointed out the address to
him.

He shook his head.

"Yes, yes," he said. "This is the place. I know. I take you."

I looked closer at the shack. It was quite obviously a store. Various canned goods were stacked on shelves along its walls. But it was hard to believe that here was the largest buyer between Cairo and Singapore of Shepherd and Gray's oil, paint, and enamel products.

It was, however.

A smile of welcome spread over the dark face of the Singalese to whom I held out my letter.

"Why, yes," he said. "From Shepherd and Gray. We hear from them. Mr. Critch he come here some while ago. We buy much from him. Now you come. Only a month later. Still we manage buy something more, I think."

"But I haven't come here to sell varnish."

"Not? But this letter you bring. From Shepherd and Gray?"

"I know. But that's just because I know them. I come as a friend."

"Come as a friend?"

He looked at me incredulously. He could not understand why any white man should come to him as a friend.

"Then you are not in Mr. Shepherd and Gray's business?" he said.

"No, no."

"Then what is your business?"

"Books."

"Boots?"

"Yes, boots," I said desperately. "I collect them."

At that he displayed no surprise.

"It must," he said, "be very interesting."

"It is. I specialise in Egyptian shoes."

He nodded, as would one connoisseur to another.

"Very interesting. Here I am afraid you will not find much. The people, you see, do not wear them."

"I know."

We looked sadly at each other. There seemed no more to be said. I got up. At that Gimvo Sanjbo looked concerned. He did not know why I had come. But I had brought a letter. I had been written about from England. I had come as a friend. Something needed to be done.

"You go now," he said. "But I like to do something for you first. I like to give you something. What can I give you?"

He looked round his tin-lined shelves. "Tea?" he said. "No, you would not want that. Some beef? Some corned beef? No, you would not like corned beef." His glance shifted from shelf to shelf despondently. I was about to put him out of his embarrassment by accepting some curried prawns when a glow of relief and pleasure lit his face. "I know," he said, "and Shepherd and Gray's own product. Some boot polish."

§

Every table was full at the G.O.H. that night when I went in to dinner. The man I was placed opposite was youthfully middle-aged. He gave the impression of having spent a good deal of his life in the tropics. There was a pint bottle of Bordeaux on the table. He introduced himself by passing it across to me.

"Help yourself," he said. "You needn't feel shy about

171

it. I'm not paying for it. It'll go down on my expense account. This is my last night in Ceylon. I'm doing myself well."

He was an auditor, he told me. An auditor of bank accounts, I gathered, though what exactly that meant I do not know. Perhaps I misunderstood him. At any rate, his job, whatever it was, involved a good deal of travel. That night he was sailing for Calcutta.

"I'll be a week there. Then Rangoon. Rangoon will be better. Less civilised. Less officious, if you understand me." He hesitated, eyeing me cautiously. "Been in the East long?" he asked.

"This is my first night in it."

He appeared relieved. "Ah, well, then you've everything to learn. Queer place, the East; swank, most of it. Look around you. All those fellows behaving as though they were lords. Haven't a penny, any of them." He leant across the table confidentially. "You take my advice. Go steady here. It's all very well swanking into the club and shouting 'Boy!' ordering rounds of drinks, signing for them as though twenty rupees weren't anything to you. At the end of the month the chits come in, and eight hundred rupees a month'll take some earning."

He spoke caustically. He was not of the public school type. I suspect that between Delhi and Colombo English society itches with class consciousness.

"Look at all these fellows," he went on. "How many of them have an anna in the bank? Why do you think they stay out here so long? Not because they love the East. You bet not. Because they can't afford to leave it. Signed too many chits. That's the trouble with them. They may give themselves airs, but how many of them," he added, producing from his waistcoat pocket a vast half-hunter, "have got a gold watch and chain?"

He dilated on the theme while we worked our way through the many-coursed and uninspired dinner. As we reached the savoury he tapped his finger against the menu. "This is all very well," he said. "But who wants to eat seven courses? A piece of steak, or a cut off the joint, with some cheese to follow. That's all I want. And that's what I'm going to have when I'm through with this. Eleven pounds a week, that's all I'll need. A little house out in Northwood, say. And I'll have my mother with me. She'll do me a better dinner than these people. That's what I'm working for. She's had a bad time, poor dear. Not much of a chap, my father. But I'll be able to make her last years good for her. Eleven pounds a week, and a little house and my mother. That's all I care about. Finished dinner? What about some billiards?"

We went.

By the time we had played our game and drunk a beer or two it was after ten. As we walked out into the empty streets a number of rickshaw men ran up to us whispering: "Missie, Missie." My companion paused.

"Three days to Calcutta, not much chance of anything on the boat. Then a day or two to find my feet. Yes, I suppose I'd better. Coming too?"

I am ready if not to taste any drink once at least to sniff its bouquet. And the night, the velvet tropic night, was propitious to adventure. Along a road starred with fireflies we were hurried towards the open country.

"Where on earth," I asked, "are we being taken?"

173

My companion laughed.

"The bishops have cleared up Colombo. One's got to go far afield nowadays."

We certainly did go far afield. We must have been travelling for a full half-hour before the rickshaws stopped in the middle of what appeared to be a large field, though, as there was no moon, it was too dark to see. There was a lot of whispering, the darkening of the rickshaw lamps, a long pause; then the sound of feet shuffling through the grass. There was more whispering. Then the apologetic voice of the rickshaw men. "One only can we find." Said my companion, "We'd better toss." I waived the right. Ten minutes later he returned. "Well, I think home," I said.

"Really? Ah, well, perhaps you're wise."

On the way back he talked to me about the house in Northwood and the dinners that his mother would cook for him on eleven pounds a week.

§

Next morning I went to Kandy. And than Kandy there can be in the world few lovelier places. There are its temples and its lake; its streets are broad, its air is cool. The Queen's Hotel is one of the best Eastern hotels that I have stayed in. I imagine that in the right mood and in the right company Kandy might be one of one's happiest travel memories. I was in neither. I had no company, and at the dawn of every day I told myself that had I remained upon the *Amboise* I should be only a few hours from Malaya and the friends who were awaiting me. The four days that I spent at Kandy were profitably industrious, but the harder one works during the day the more does one need congenial companionship during the evening.

I returned in a disgruntled temper to find Colombo intolerably hot and crowded with festivity. It was the week when the Governor's Cup was run for, when Up Country played Colombo at Rugby football, and many of the young men from the plantations were in town. With a jaundiced eye I watched them filling the hotels with exuberant, self-conscious self-assertion. A sorrier exhibition I thought I had not ever seen. Here, it seemed to me, were a number of undistinguished people of no account in their own country, who possessed no qualities that would entitle them in their own country to recognition and esteem, behaving as if they were feudal chieftains for no better reason than that their parents had happened to be whites. I know now that I was wrong to form that estimate of them, that people must be seen in their own setting, that my judgment of the young planters of Ceylon was as unfocussed as would have been during the war an attempt to appraise the qualities of the temporary officer as a man and a soldier on his behaviour in the lounge of the Regent Palace Hotel.

I counted the hours to the sailing of the *Angers*. When she arrived, however, except for the fact that I was being carried by her to Singapore, I would just as soon have been at Kandy. At no time can the *Angers* be a pleasant ship. German originally, she is cumbersome and ill-appointed. Second-class passengers, though their meals are served separately, occupy the same deck as the first-class passengers, with the result that the decks are uncomfortably crowded. There was not, for example, a deck-chair available when I got on board. It would need cheery company to make a trip on the *Angers* enjoyable. And cheeriness is not a characteristic of French ships. The French people carry on to their ships the exclusiveness of their domestic lives. They are not easy or welcoming of approach. When you board an English ship in the middle of her run, before you have eaten your first meal, the secretary of the sports committee has entered your name for innumerable competitions. "Why can't these people let me alone?" you think, as you wait till the saloon is empty to pass your opponents into the second round. But on that trip I would have been grateful for egg and spoon races and deck quoits and rings. During the six days between Colombo and Singapore I spoke to one man only, and not to him except at meals. I counted the minutes to Singapore.

But Singapore can be a frightening city. To the stranger most cities are. It is big and busy. The rickshaw boys speak no English, and you feel forlornly helpless as you try to explain to them where you want to go in English that you imagine will be more comprehensible if you pidgin it. As they hurry you through the wide clean streets you have no confidence that they are understanding you. Under any circumstances I should have been glad when the *Kinta* sailed for Penang at four o'clock. As it was, I was to count the seconds. For in a mood of unreflecting folly I bought myself four silk shirts; and it was not till I was sipping a lime-squash in the lounge of the "Europe" that I discovered that I had in my pocket barely enough money to buy a ticket and get down to the steamer, and that as it was on a Penang bank that I was authorised to cash cheques I had no means of getting any more.

"That's pretty silly of me," I thought. "It looks as though I shall have to miss my lunch."

The thought did not particularly worry me. I had eaten a late and ample breakfast; in the tropics the less one eats the better. I sat back in my chair contentedly reading the account of the last Test Match. It was not till the tables round me began to fill that I started to wonder how and where I was to put in the time between now and the sailing of my ship. It was twelve o'clock. The ferry left at three. Three hours had to be filled in somehow. I had nowhere in which to spend them, no room, no club, no flat, no place in the whole town in which I should be justified in sitting without payment. I had never realised before the extent to which we hire everything. It is not only flats we rent. We rent for an hour with a quart of beer the wooden stool of a publichouse, with a cocktail the small table of the "Trocadero" bar, with a lunch the green and gilt of the "Berkeley." Dejectedly I wondered for how long I should have been held to have rented my chair in the lounge of the "Europe" for a ten-cent lime-squash.

The lounge was rapidly becoming full. Newcomers paused in the doorway searching carefully for an empty table. As a marooned sailor watches the tide come in, I saw chair after vacant chair appropriated. Now there were only two free tables. Now there was only one. Now that had gone. There were only scattered here and there a spare chair or two. And I at my table was occupying four with a solitary glass of lime-squash upon the table. And all the time people were coming in. A

177

waiter was eyeing me with distrust. "Who," he was saying to himself, "is this wretched stranger who is keeping a whole table to himself, robbing me of tips and custom?" Every moment I grew more uncomfortable. "I must go," I thought. "It's no good. I've got to go." One's purse has to be full before one can enslave a waiter. I left the hotel in such confusion that on the way I handed the cloakroom attendant a one-cent tip.

It was only half-past twelve. Out of a cloudless sky an equatorial sun was blazing. Heat and glare quivered from the stone pavements and the yellow buildings. I had not walked ten yards before I had begun to feel my shoulders damp against my shirt. For two hours and a half I had to endure that heat and glare. Singapore is a brave city, a brave and lovely city, with fine streets and stately buildings, a broadly curving, sampan-covered river, and Chinese shops with gold lettering on black. But it is no city for a white man's patrolling between the hours of half-past twelve and three. Those two and a half hours were in all that unsatisfactory month to which they were the climax, the most wretched. I do not know how I spent them. I loitered before shop windows. I escaped out of the heat into the shadowed cool of a bookshop, making enquiries about such books as they were the least likely to possess, dreading that they might possess them; turning the pages of a magazine, suspecting that at any moment a voice would thunder behind my ear, "If you want to buy that magazine, then buy it. If not, go out!" I know nothing that reduces one's morale more effectively than an empty pocket. One feels at the mercy of any one who chooses to insult one. I counted the seconds to the sailing of the *Kinta*.

And it was a moment worth counting seconds to, a moment of utter contrast. It was a neat and dapper boat. Clean and polished after the uncarpeted passages of the *Angers*; small and intimate after the strangeness of unfamiliar places. English was being talked instead of French. There was a pleasant young Irishman with whom I immediately fell into conversation. I felt myself at home again. With all my troubles at the back of me. Thirty-six hours away Penang was waiting; and at Penang there would be friends and a bank account. I lay back in a long chair utterly at peace. I have rarely known a moment of more complete relief.

Usually it is to such moments of anticipation that one's memory returns with the greatest fondness. However disenchanting the place or meeting that one has counted the seconds to may prove to be, one can always look back and say, "Well, anyhow, there was that moment when the liner sailed, when the bustling little tugs berthed the vast ship against the docks, when the train puffed slowly from the station. At any rate, I had those moments." In this case, however, fate was charitable, and the sailing of the *Kinta* was not only the curtain upon a series of exacting circumstances—it was the prelude to two of the best months I have ever known. Malaya and Penang were not to belie anything that I had ever dreamt of them.

THE ENGLISHMAN IN THE TROPICS

VII

WITH the exception of Tahiti, I was never sorrier to leave any place than I was Penang. It is not easy to explain, however, why my stay there was so happy. In the same way that it is more difficult for the novelist to depict a sympathetic than an unsympathetic character, it is easier to show why you dislike than why you like a place. And the charm of Penang is made the harder to convey by the fact that for the Englishman all places out of England governed by Englishmen are superficially the same. As it is in Malay, so it is in the Caribbean.

Most of the passenger traffic in the West Indies is of a tourist nature. You either work down the islands to Demerara from Halifax or New York, or, sailing straight from Europe, you make a circular trip along the South American coast to Colon and back *via* Jamaica. The ships stop for from six to thirty-six hours at the various ports. Excursions are arranged for the passengers. They are met by cars. They are driven across the island. The beauty spots and historical sites are pointed out to them. They bathe. They take photographs. They acquire souvenirs. The local hotel provides them with an ill-served meal, considerably inferior to the lunch they would have had on board. In the life of the island they never mix. And when they discuss, after a five hours' acquaintanceship with each, the difference between Antigua, Nevis and St. Kitts, "The great thing about the islands," they will say, "is that every one of them is different."

Which they are, of course, if you visit them that way.

It would be simple to write a travel book on the West Indies—a number of people have—which would give the impression that no two islands are alike. Antigua is dry and flattish on the leeward coast. Hills, green with sugar-cane, climb gently backward from a beach so white that the sea above it assumes the most exquisite and varied shades of colour. The town is sleepy. Its streets are wide and clean and empty. Indolent negroes lounge in the doorways of their huts and shout at you as you go past. The sole people with any apparent commercial enterprise are the small boys who hold out their hands and beg for a black penny. Nothing seems to be happening. My hotel bedroom looked down on to the main street. It was so quiet that I might have fancied myself in the wilds of Wiltshire.

Nowhere in the world will you find better bathing. A mile out of St. John, by a ruined fort whose guns once commanded the entrance to the harbour, there are neat cabins and a café where you can dance; and it is past a pleasant lawn, through a well-kept garden, that you stroll to a white, gently sloping beach, where there are neither rocks nor coral, where you swim out through pale blue water to a raft.

History has lingered at Antigua. From Clarence House you look down on to the harbour where the fleets that chased Villeneuve across the Atlantic anchored. They say, though history scarcely supports the claim, that Nelson re-fitted here before Trafalgar. Certainly, in his early days he spent many months in the wooden house whose timber is now cracked and porous. For decades of years the yellow and crumbling barracks were filled with bluejackets, with the sound of drilling feet, with the laughter of men at play. The stones in the graveyard carry the names of many soldiers. On Shirley Heights you will find ranged among weeds the stone ruins of orderly room and mess-room, the moss-grown gun emplacements that watched the enemy outline of Guadeloupe, the vast cistern that husbanded the scanty supply of rain.

That is how the five-hours' visitor will see Antigua.

To such a one no place could seem more different than Dominica. It is mountainous: so mountainous that the towering hills seem to be pushing the little town of Roseau into the sea. There are no roads across the island. The sand is black. The water is grey or darkly blue. There is no bathing. The piers and bathing huts have been swept away by hurricanes. The town is bright and noisy. Picturesquely-dressed girls chatter in French patois to one another. It is always raining.

South of Dominica there is Saint Lucia. From Martinique you see its twin, cone-shaped Pitons. The ship will not stay there for more than a few hours. You will have no time to do more than drive up into the hills and look down on to the bay, on to the ships at anchor, on to the midget town of Castries, and wonder whether Naples is any finer. Next morning you will reach Barbados.

Barbados is as flat as Antigua and no larger. It is the most densely-populated island in the world, and perhaps the ugliest. Bridgetown is hot and noisy. The glare from the streets is dazzling. Except in the north of the island, by Bathseba, you will drive through flat fields of sugar-cane. Not a foot of ground is wasted. You will wonder how any one ever finds his way about. Every road looks the same. There are no sign posts. There are no landmarks. The road which one morning will be high with sugar-cane will be unrecognisable when the crop has been removed. The thirty-six hours' tourist will make for the pier of the Aquatic Club and will not leave it till the last syren of his steamer hoots.

The Aquatic Club is the perfect playground. It is not really a club, since any one who is not black can join it. You become a member for a day, a week, a year. It is a pier running out some fifty yards into the sea. There are tennis courts at its base, and cabins and a souvenir shop. There is a dancing hall and above it a tar-floored roof which the sun worshippers have appropriated. Its atmosphere is rather like that of the hot-room of a Turkish bath. No notice excluding women has been posted, but at all hours of the day you will find its benches strewn with tanned and naked forms. At the head of the pier there is the club house. There is a bar, there are lunch tables, there is a dancing floor. There are diving boards and water shoots and trapezes. And as you swim a gramophone is playing, and young people are shouting and laughing to one another. The sun shines. Every one is carefree, happy, at ease. Time does not exist.

Trinidad is a twelve-hour journey from Barbados. You feel as though you were coming into a different world when you wake in the morning and see, green and high on either side of you, the outline of the Bocas. You anchor a mile or so away from Port of Spain, and the hills are so high that in relation to them you fancy that there is no more than a village awaiting you at their foot. The size of Port of Spain astonishes you. It is like no other town in the West Indies. Straight, wide and clean, the streets run from the savannah to the sea, their uniformity contrasting curiously with the polyglot population that throngs its sidewalks. Every people of the world seems to be represented here. There are Indian women in long white robes, their noses pierced with gold and brass decorations. There are Chinese signs over the shops. There are notices in Spanish. There are the inevitable negroes. There are many French. Trinidad has passed through several hands. The outline of Venezuela is only seven miles away.

It is a rich and fertile island. Ninety-five per cent. of the world's asphalt comes from there. The roads are smooth and wide over which you drive through landscape infinitely varied and infinitely lovely. There are cane fields and plains of coconut. In the hills the scarlet of the immortelle shelters and shadows the immature cocoa growth. In the south there is the barren stretch of the pitch lake and the wooden derricks of the oil-fields. From Trinidad comes all the Angostura of the world.

Few products have a more romantic history.

A hundred years ago, in South America, a Dr. Siegert produced a blend of aromatic and tonic bitters that he called "Aromatic Bitters." It was produced as a medicine solely, and it is as a medicine that it appears on the tariff of the United States, although 90 per cent. of its contents are honest rum. It was made by Dr. Siegert for circulation among his friends and patients. It was not till its success led to exportation that it was christened "Angostura" after the town where at that time the doctor was head-quartered, and where his factory remained till the un-settled condition of Venezuelan politics counselled a move to Trinidad. To-day the concoction that was devised as a cure for diarrhœa is the flavouring of 90 per cent. of the world's cocktails. A million bottles are exported yearly. The secret of its ingredients has never been divulged. Only three men, the three partners, know them. They do the mixing of it personally in their laboratory. Chemists are unable to diagnose its consistent parts. They recognise that one out of five drugs has been employed, but they do not know which. Till they can find out there will remain only one Angostura. No history of the West Indies would be complete that did not contain a chapter on it. In the West Indies it is employed as no one would think of em-ploying it in Europe. In England a bottle of Angostura will last about a year. In the West Indies they use a tea-spoonful and a half at least to every cocktail. Every cocktail is coloured pink. They are described as dry or sweet, and the Englishman who orders a dry cocktail will get the surprise of his life when he tastes the pale pink liquid with its creaming froth. Particularly if he sips at it; for the West Indian custom is to finish your cocktail at a single swallow. Perhaps that is the only way dry cocktails can be drunk. I never got the habit, and until I had learnt to ask for sugar in my cocktail I used to maintain that the West Indian variety looked the best and tasted the worst of any in the world. If you want to know what one is like the coloured barman at the small bar in the "Trocadero" will mix you one. He came from the Siegert factory. And to take the taste out of your mouth afterwards he will shake you a Green Swizzle, a Trinidadian drink that, as far as I know, you won't find anywhere else this side of the Atlantic.

Then there is the hotel. I am not sure that the "Baracuda" does not deserve to be the subject of a novel as much as the "Grand Babylon." It is the hotel of legend, the hotel that people have in the back of their minds as a popular conception when they ask the traveller, "But the hotels—isn't all that part of it rather unpleasant? The discomfort, the dirt, the noise."

At a first sight there is nothing to tell that it is going to be that kind of place. It looks out on to the wide savannah and the high hills that shelter it. It has a drive marked "In" and "Out." There is a largish and cool verandah. There are notices of billiard rooms, dancing rooms and baths. There is a souvenir store. And at the desk a large, brass-bound book that swivels round for you to sign your name in. You are charged six dollars for an average room. You are reminded of Raffles, of the "Galle Face" and the

"E and O." It is not till you reach your room that suspicion comes to you. It is only a suspicion. Tropical hotels are furnished barely. There is the bed with its white mosquito net. There is a washstand, a chest of drawers, a table, a couple of wooden chairs, a mat or so. You cannot make much out of material of that kind. But there was an ill-omened atmosphere of unkemptness about that room. Two minutes later the suspicion had deepened.

"I'd better have a look at the baths," I said.

I was conducted down some hundred and fifty feet of passage. There were a number of corners along the road. It was like being taken through a maze. At the end of the passage was the lavatory and two bathrooms that served some twenty rooms.

"But, look here," I said, "I'll never be able to find this again. Is there nothing nearer?"

The bell boy shook his head.

"There's a shower bath downstairs," he said. "You go through the billiard room and turn to the right past the bar, and then—"

But that was too complicated. "Never mind," I said. "You run along and bring me up an inkpot."

I went back to my room and began unpacking. Quarter of an hour later my clean linen had been separated from my dirty, but I lacked the ink with which to prepare my laundry list. I rang the bell. After some delay the door handle was rattled. There was a pause; then a tap on the door. "Come in," I called out. "Door's locked," the answer came. "It isn't," I shouted. Again the door handle rattled: again ineffectively. "Oh, all right," I said, and opened the door myself. A bell boy was standing in the doorway. He looked at the lock resentfully. "Door stick," he explained to me.

"I know," I said. "Now run and fetch an inkpot."

He stared and repeated the word "inkpot." Then went out, leaving the door unshut. I got up and shut it. For five minutes nothing happened. Then there was a rattle at the door. "Come in," I called. "Door locked," the answer came. "Oh, no," I said, "it isn't. You try again." Again the handle rattled. Finally it gave. Another bell boy was standing in the doorway.

"That fellow new here," he said. "What is it you want?"

I told him. He nodded intelligently, then went, leaving the door open, to return two minutes later with an empty inkpot.

My room was in the corner of the wall, with Eldred's at right angles to it. It was quite easy for us to talk across to one another.

"What do you think of this place?" I said.

"That it's lucky," he answered, "we haven't the siesta habit."

It was. We should never have been able to sleep there during the day time. The noise was incessant. Every car that passed in front of the hotel—and some two hundred cars passed every hour—honked its horn both at the "In" and "Out" opening of the drive.

"The less time," said Eldred, "that we spend in this hotel the better. Let's go for a drive."

We returned shortly after twelve to find every table in the verandah occupied, every passage crowded, and an

189

alert custodian at the doorway of the dining-room with a demand for tickets.

We stared blankly. "Tickets? What tickets?"

"Lunch tickets."

It sounded like a return of the days of rationing. "Lunch tickets?" we repeated.

"Yes, these," and he produced from a desk a number of green perforated slips across which had been printed "Universal Tourist Bureau. Trinidad. Lunch, Baracuda Hotel. Tips included." And stamped across it the name of the ship, S.S. *Reputed*.

Then we understood.

"But we're staying here," we said.

"Oh, in that case"—he still looked dubious, however—"there's a tourist boat in, and when that happens we like our guests to breakfast early."

For in Trinidad meals follow the plantation routine. Tea between six and eight; breakfast between eleven and half-past twelve. "I'm afraid," he said, "that you'll find it rather a squash in there."

That was not the way in which I should have described it. The dining-room looked like Point à Pitré after the cyclone had passed over it. Four hundred people had been or were being served with lunch. The few empty tables were covered with soiled cloths, dirty plates, dry glasses. The people who were sitting at the other tables were in tune with the atmosphere. Their faces were flushed; their manners boisterous; their glasses were half full, which is to say that they were themselves completely. It took us a long time to attract attention to ourselves. Then the wine waiter bustled up.

"What would you like to drink?" he said.

"We want a table."

"I know, but what would you like to drink?"

During the twenty minutes that we waited for a clean tablecloth and clean plates to be set five wine waiters approached us. On boat days all available bell boys became ganymedes.

Eventually we were served with lunch. Personally, I thought the food less bad than popular report considers it. The menu varies little. There is grapefruit. There is a fish called salmon. There are some Venezuelan patties. There are cold meats. There is roast turkey. If you ask for anything that is not on the menu they will try to charge you extra. One evening I asked for three fried eggs instead of the set dinner, and found that forty-eight cents had been charged against me on the bill. The food is less varied and less well-cooked than at the small boarding-house hotels of the Leeward Islands, but, at the same time, it is not so bad as the majority of residents maintain it to be. The Venezuelan patties were quite good.

"How often do you have these boats in?" we asked our waiter.

"Every few days," he told us, "in the season."

Immediately after lunch we left the hotel. We did not return to it till half-past eleven. The noise had in no way abated. There was a tourist dance in progress. The hotel is constructed of thin wood: you can hear everything that is said and done in the room next door. Every beat of the foxtrot can be heard in every corner of the fabric.

"Heaven knows," said Eldred, "how we shall get to sleep."

I was so exhausted, however, after a night at sea, after a long day of sun amid the strain of new contacts, that in spite of the noise I was asleep within five minutes.

It was not for long: cars were still honking their horns in the street, feet were pattering down passages, whispered "Good-nights" were being prolonged over banisters, when I woke out of a nightmare, my face stung and swollen. The briefest examination of my sheets sufficed. I rang the bell.

"Bed bugs," I told the boy.

He stared. "Such a thing has never happened in this hotel," he said.

"It has now," I said. "Look there!"

His sight convinced him. "I will fetch the maid," he said.

A weary-eyed wench arrived. "Bed bugs," I told her.

"Such a thing has never happened in this hotel," she said.

I pointed to the sheets, and sat gloomily by while they and the pillow slips were changed.

"It will be all right now," she said.

It wasn't. I had scarcely begun to doze before a fierce stab in the throat sent me raging into the passage. There was a bell boy collecting shoes.

"Hi!" I shouted. "Bugs are biting me!"

"Bugs!"

"Bed bugs."

"Ah!"

He stood staring, his arms full of shoes.

"I want another mattress," I said.

"Too late," he answered, and prepared to go downstairs.

"Then get me another room."

"Too late," he said, his foot on the top stair.

But I was not letting him escape.

"Either I am found a new room," I said, "or I will leave the hotel to-morrow, which will probably mean the sack for you."

By that time I imagine that any one in the hotel who was not snoringly asleep must have been aroused. I expected to see doors flung open down the passage. I wondered how the laws of Trinidad were constituted. I wondered whether there was such a thing as criminal slander; whether I could be sued for it on the grounds that my revelations on the bug-fed beds had occasioned a breach of the public peace. The bell boy, however, had a dislike of scenes.

I was got my room. It was a reasonable room. An eight or ten dollar room. I slept deep and late. Eldred, however, who was kept awake by the music till after one, was woken every twenty minutes by different bell boys from half-past six onwards with the news that my door was locked and that no answer could be got to knocks.

"When," he asked, "did you say that the next boat for Jamaica leaves?"

That morning we discussed seriously the problem of searching for a new hotel. There were many disadvantages. We had sent a good deal of linen to the laundry. We had given the "Baracuda" as our address. By the time our friends had realised that we had moved we should have ourselves moved from Trinidad. After all, it was only for a week.

And there is a satisfaction, too, in making the worst of

a bad job. When twenty consecutive June days have been spoilt by rain you are almost irritated when the sun shines upon the twenty-first. You want a record for bad Junes to be established. In the same way, we took the "Baracuda" as a grisly joke. We would have bets as to how long it would take to get anything we wanted.

"I am going to ring for my bath now," I would call across to Eldred. "You be timekeeper."

The game had to be played under strict rulings. If you asked simply for a bath, you could not claim a victory on the grounds that there was no water in it. It was a long job to get a bath. There was no system by which you rang once for a maid, twice for a bell boy, three times for iced water. When you rang a bell boy arrived. He would take a minute or so to open the door. You would ask him to send the maid along. He would leave the door open when he went out, and time was wasted while he was being summoned back to close it. If nothing happened within five minutes the rule decreed that you must ring again. Almost certainly it would be a different boy who would answer you. You would explain that you had asked for your maid to be sent to you. He would explain that it was a new boy who did not know his way about whom you had asked. He himself would see to it. And he would leave the door open when he went. Eventually your maid would arrive. "Can I have a bath?" you would ask. Certainly: she would send the bath maid. Then there was a question of towels and of soap. A lengthy process. The worst time was thirteen minutes, the best three-quarters of an hour.

We relaxed. We never made an attempt to go to sleep

before one o'clock. We danced as long as there was dancing. And when dancing ceased we would drive up Chancellor's Road, count the cars suspiciously parked in ditches, or race along the coast-line to the little Church of St. Peter and argue as to the locality of the Southern Cross. We saw to it that our car should be the last car to honk by the savannah and our good-night the last to echo down the corridor. We made the worst of a bad job. We were a-weary, though, at the end of it. And on the last evening we decided that, since we could not sleep early in the evening, we would try if we could not sleep late in the morning. Our own waiter was away, but to his deputy we gave the clearest orders that Eldred was to be called at nine and myself at eight. On our return from Chancellor's Road at two o'clock we repeated our instructions to the night porter. He assured us there should be no mistake. He took down our names and numbers. He chalked up the hours on the board. Eldred at nine; myself at eight.

Things ended as they had begun.

Keatings and a new mattress had cleaned my bed. They could not strengthen a feeble fabric. As I got into bed, three of the springs gave way, and with a loud crack the mattress collapsed on its iron support. There was silence. Then from Eldred's window came a cackle of horrid laughter. An instant later every one in that section of the hotel must have been awake. On my wall and on Eldred's fists were beaten, and furious voices were adjuring us to remember that there were other people in the hotel besides ourselves. We refrained from arguments. It took us half an hour to make my bedstead possible. "Thank heavens I told them to call me late," I thought as I pulled the coverlet round me.

I ought to have known better.

Punctually at seven o'clock I was awoken by a clattered tray.

I made no protest. I got up and drank my tea, ate my toast, and sat with my head nodding, my eyelids heavy, waiting for eight o'clock, for the tap upon Eldred's door, the clink of plates and for Eldred's indignant protest of "Oh, really!"

I did not wait in vain.

§

AFTER TRINIDAD, JAMAICA

Jamaica is the largest and most famous of the British Antilles, and those who think of the West Indies as one place link it mentally with Barbados and Trinidad. Actually, in point of time it is further away from Port of Spain than Chicago is from London. There is no way of getting to it in under seven days, and when ultimately you arrive there by means of Costa Rica and Panama, you might fancy you were arriving in another continent. It is large and it is rich. So large that you feel, as you scarcely can feel in the other islands, that it is possible to lead a private life without interference. Pounds and not dollars are the currency, but the island is managed very largely by the United Fruit Company, an American organisation that owns the ships that connect it with England and America, and that have built large hotels on the American plan and on the American tariff. Tourists are admirably catered for. It is the one island at which a visitor could enjoy himself without knowing the residents, the one island where there is a satisfactory tourist information bureau. Within two hours of our arrival we found ourselves with a motoring licence and an agreeable Oakland. To enjoy Jamaica a motor car is essential. Such bathing as exists is poor. Only Montego Bay can compare with Barbados and Antigua. Jamaica's chief attraction is its scenery. Parts of it are unrivalled. When you look down from Hardware Gap and see Kingston through an avenue of hills, smouldering and glittering in the plain, you feel that just this once the Almighty has pulled his stuff to show the scenic decorators where they get off. The conditions for motoring are perfect. The actual surface of the roads is better in Trinidad and in Malaya, but in compensation for that you have all over the island pleasant little townships, the majority of which have clean and relatively inexpensive hotels at which you can break your journey. Motoring in the tropics is usually complicated by the absence of hotels and resting houses. In Jamaica there are no such difficulties. You can travel at hazard. During our three weeks there we followed the road as it chose to wind.

§

No islands could seemingly be more different, one from the other. But to the Englishman superficially they will seem the same. The English carry their own lives with them. They make no attempt to assimilate into the character of the countries that they occupy. The British troops who entered Cologne after the war behaved as though there were no Germans there at all. They carried on with their own routine of training and athletics as if they were at Aldershot or Salisbury Plain. In the same spirit have the English colonised India, the Antilles and the Far East. An Englishman living in Penang is as little affected by the presence round him of the Malays, the Tamils, and the Chinese as is his elder brother in South Kensington by the slums that are west of Hammersmith.

An Englishman arriving at an English-governed community knows precisely what is awaiting him. He will present his letters of introduction, and immediately he will be received into the life of the community. He becomes a part of whatever fun is going. He becomes a member of the clubs. Wherever two or three Englishmen are gathered together a club is formed. I recall a plantation club in the F.M.S. that consisted of three members: the president, the vice-president, and the honorary secretary. The club met every evening; each member called for two rounds of drinks, signed for them, and at the end of the month received his bill. There are usually two kinds of club: there is the men's club, a bridge and drinking club very largely; and there is the mixed club, which combines golf and tennis. It is the mixed club that marks the main difference between English and French colonial life. After a couple of months in Martinique I am still as ignorant as when I went there as to what constitutes the life of the Frenchwoman. I do not know where she goes or what she does. There is no tennis club, there is no dance club. The bathing beaches are empty. Occasionally one or two of them would join their husbands on the ground floor of the

club. Upstairs they are not allowed. Once I went to a jol-
lyish flappers' dance; once a fleet of cars arrived outside our
bungalow and a number of young men and women drank
some punch and danced on the verandah. Apart from
that I did not receive a single intimation that the men
whom I met at the Club were not sisterless and motherless
bachelors. The French, I know, keep their home life very
closely to themselves. But even so I cannot imagine how
their women folk pass their time. I cannot believe that
they really spend their entire lives darning socks indoors.

French colonial life centres round the home. English
colonial life centres round its club. The gaiety of the day
is concentrated into those three hours between five and
eight when the offices are closed and the air has begun to
cool. For an hour or an hour and a half while the light
lasts there is golf and tennis; then there is a gathering on
the verandah of the club house. There is a rattling of
ice on glass. An hour or so of chatter that grows livelier as
the glasses empty. Gradually the throng diminishes. For
some there are dinner parties waiting. But for the majority the life of the day is ended when silence settles on the
verandah. Dinner is a rushed meal. One is to bed early.

That is the routine, the framework of the day. There
are variations, naturally. There are excursions and there
are parties. The accounts of colonial hospitality are not
exaggerated. You are regarded as a guest. And the members of the community see to it that you enjoy yourself.
As it was in Penang, so it was in the Antilles. And though
I have never been to Western Africa, I am tolerably sure
of what it would be like. There would be the club, the
games, the parties, the formalities of book-signing and

card-leaving. When you have seen one English community you have seen the lot. Superficially, that is to say.

But it would need a traveller more experienced than I to describe how differences of climate and nationality have changed and modified the character of the English life that has been superimposed on them. I can recognise that there are differences between the English in Malaya and Siam, between the English in Barbados and Trinidad and Dominica. But I do not know enough, I have not seen enough to diagnose those differences, to explain what they are and how they have come about. I can only describe in broad outline the difference between the Far East and the Antilles.

The difference is very great. It is the difference between Europe and America, between an old civilisation and a new. Though that is not an exact parallel, because one of the chief differences between Malaya and the Antilles is that, whereas the West Indians have been born and will die beside the Caribbean, the English go to Malaya for fifteen, for twenty, for thirty years to make the money on which they will retire. The West Indian speaks of England as "home" as the Australian speaks of England as "home." Half his life is spent in planning for a holiday in England, but his roots are in the West Indies. Whereas the Englishman in the Far East has his roots in England; he talks not of a "holiday" but of "leave"; he is working for the day when he will take his farewell for ever of the rubber trees and rice-fields and the brown and friendly rivers. He is a pioneer, and his is the life vigorous and optimistic of the pioneer. He is building into the future. And it is this that makes one compare in its essentials life in the Far

East with life in America. Both are pioneer. They are living in the future. They have no past. The present is something that is to be scraped in a few years' time. The Americans do not build motor cars that will last a lifetime. They do not want things that will last a lifetime. In a few years greater knowledge and facilities will have produced better models. We are told that the Americans think about nothing except money, though this criticism does not come too well from a class that spends a third of its time discussing death duties, income tax, the cost of living and servants' wages. But the American only likes money because there is so much for him to buy with it. The American attitude to money is different from the European. When an American is in debt it is because he is living upon a shoe-string; he has bought up shares and real estate because he had the money handy for the first instalment, but finds the meeting of the subsequent instalments is beyond his means. The American mortgages his future, the Englishman more often mortgages his past. He arranges a reversion. He sells or borrows money on a section of his property. He draws upon his capital. The American in anticipating his income is forced to realise his potentialities. In Europe, at every street corner, in every old building, you are being reminded of the past. You are having it suggested to you that the best is over. In America every new story and every new skyscraper is a vindication of what lies ahead. I have returned to London devitalised from a month among the walled cities of old Tuscany. But America is like a strong wind blowing through you. It is in the last analysis this atmosphere of optimism, of looking forward, that makes me so happy in America, and among Americans. And it is because I found this atmosphere in Malaya that I prefer Malaya to the Antilles.

§

The West Indies have known many varying fortunes. They were our first colonial possessions, and for two centuries they were the most prosperous. In those days such phrases as "rich as a West Indian," and "working like a nigger," were in common use. The islands were so rich that many of their owners lived in England on their revenues, leaving their estates to be mismanaged and their slaves ill-used by overseers. Then slavery ended and sugar slumped. There was competition from the subsidised beet industry. Then Java came into the market, then Cuba. And though there have been revivals, though even during the last decade fortunes have been made in sugar, each wave of depression has meant the bankruptcy of proprietors, the sale, and as often as not the splitting up of properties, with noble houses crumbling into rubble. The Old West Indian life is passing.

And it was a fine life. How fine can be best realised in Barbados.

Barbados is to the thirty-six-hour tourist the least attractive island in the Antilles. It is the most to those who stay long enough to see something of its life. It is the oldest and the most English colony. Geographically, apart from the other islands, it has remained Englishly self-contained. The colour line has been retained there. Its history does carry few blemishes of tyranny and ill-usage. During three hundred years it has built up traditions and a culture of its own. You have the feeling of a family life firmly and surely built—as firmly and surely built as the strong, thick-walled, stone houses in which the traditions of colonial hospitality have been sustained. There are many lovely houses in Barbados. The rooms are filled with old pictures and old furniture. There is much entertaining, and the long polished tables gleam with old silver and cut glass. You do not feel that you are in a colony. You feel that this life here is as old as England. And as you close your eyes there rises before you the picture of the world that Père Labat wrote of: that elegant and extravagant prosperity that during the last hundred years has been drifting northward and eastward further and further, year by year.

There is a wistful quality about Barbados. Something of that same wistfulness with which in England you watch the conversion of old country houses into schools and sanatoria and country clubs. And there is not here as there is in England the reassuring prosperity of the north, the new streets like Kingsway; the new buildings like Carreras, the witnesses that there is a confident future in rivalry to the past. The future of the West Indies is obscure. For forty, for fifty years the pessimists have been prophesying their bankruptcy. And although some intervention of Providence has on each occasion staved off disaster, the sea has all the time been cutting in. There is no longer a future for the young man in the West Indies. The young man with ambition will go to Canada or New York or Europe. He does not see how sugar can give him the life to which his ambition entitles him. At one time there was the suggestion made that the West Indies should be

ceded to America in settlement of the debt. A suggestion
that must have made any one smile who knew anything of
the West Indies. One might as well talk of ceding the isles
of Man and Wight. Besides, it is not on America but on
Canada that the islands are dependent. The West Indies
will remain British. Whether or not they will remain English is another matter.

It is, perhaps, an impertinence for one whose acquaintance with the Antilles is so brief to prophesy on matters
over which experts have exercised themselves so much.
But the opinion of every independent witness seems to be
that the future prosperity of the West Indies lies not with
the big plantation, but with groups of peasant proprietors
linked by systems of co-operative marketing; that it lies not
with the white but with the coloured man. In some
islands, Grenada and Tobago for example, the change has
already come. In every island except Antigua and Barbados the colour line is overlooked. In Trinidad and Jamaica
the man who looks white is white. In the West Indies, as in
Europe, it is no longer profitable to look far back into a
man's antecedents. Each man stands on his own achieve-
ment. At the moment the coloured man is incapable of
self-government. Haiti is a proof of that. And it would
seem that the job of the purely white man in the West
Indies is to hold the fort till the brown man is capable
of running his own show. In fifty years I suspect that
most of the land will have passed into the hands of coloured
men, that the position of the pure white will be what the
position of the American is in Haiti, administrative and
advisory.

To wander to-day through the Antilles is rather like

reading the last chapter of a Galsworthy novel. It is a period of transition. An era is passing. There was good in the old ways. Change is no less sad for being inevitable. Appropriately enough it was in Dominica that I met a character as Galsworthian as Swithin Forsyte.

§

Before Eldred Curwen and I were five days out of Bordeaux we had heard about him. He was one of those figures round whom legends grow. "What, going to Dominica? Well, then, you must be sure to go and see the judge. He's the most original thing the islands have produced."

"In what way original?" we asked.

And heads would be nodded and anecdotes retailed, and gradually from this person and that the facts of his life took shape. He was an Englishman, the son of a West Country solicitor, who as a young boy had been sent to Antigua for convalescence after a long illness. He stayed a year, and when the time came for him to go he was so silent that his friends looked inquiringly at him.

"Are you as sad as all that to say good-bye?" they asked.

"I'm not saying good-bye," he answered. "I'm coming back."

They laughed at that. So many people had said they were coming back. So few had. "In England you'll forget us quickly enough," they said.

He didn't, though. During his three years at Oxford, where he rowed in his college boat, and in London afterwards, where he was studying for the Bar, his resolve to return strengthened. He was home-sick for the Antilles, for the sunlit skies, for the green spears of the young cane, for the yellow sands, and the sea turquoise and green above them. But it was not only for the obvious beauties that he was homesick, for sunlit and moonlit skies, for warm seas and heavy scents. In London, where the rain beats round windy corners he listened vainly for the sound of wind and rain, for the drum-beat of rain upon the palm frond and the corrugated iron roofs, for the wail of wind upon the jagged leaves of the banana. It was not only the sunlight that he was longing for. "I must hear rain again," he said. At the age of twenty-seven he sailed for the countries of the typhoon.

He has never left them. To-day, forty years later, an old man, his life's work over, he lives on the windward coast of Dominica, on an estate that just pays its way, with a retired Army captain who came out to him as a pupil and stayed on. He has been there for eight years and he will never leave it. Roseau is seven hours away; seven hours of rough and hilly riding; a journey that he would be too heavy now, even if he had the wish, which he has not, to make. "I shall never leave here," he says.

Round such a figure inevitably legends grow. And during his young and middle years he gave ample opportunity for the spreading of many legends. He was a just judge and fine lawyer. No one has ever questioned that. But he was a fighter. He bore fools ill. He stood no nonsense from officialdom. When people irritated him, he let them know it. They were his intellectual inferiors. His rapier was the sharper. He made enemies. He made friends. He had the belligerence of a man who knows his mind. The generosity of a man who is unafraid. "He's on a big scale," they told me.

It was in a mixed mood that we set out to see him, as the result of some vague telephonic talk. We were curious to see him, but a little nervous as to the reception that awaited us.

"At any rate," said Eldred, "we'll see something of the country."

Dominica has been called the loveliest of the Antilles. In a way it is. It is very mountainous. It is very green. It has not the parched barbaric thrill of Guatemala nor the terrifying austerity of the Blue Mountains of New South Wales. But, of their kind, its succession of deep gorges is as good as anything I have seen. It is rather like a reading of *Endymion*: like *Endymion* it is lush and featureless; like *Endymion* it becomes monotonous. Hour after hour it is the same. You descend hills and you mount them. At the foot of each valley, wherever a stream is running into the sea, you will find a group of native girls washing their clothes. In Dominica the negro type is purified by a Carib strain; the hair is straight and black, the features finer, the hands and feet less squat. As you pass they wave their hands and shout you friendly greetings in Creole *patois*. Occasionally you will pass a village: a collection of fishing huts beside the sea. You will pass no big houses, no sign of extensive cultivation. Here and there you will come across the ruined masonry of wall and house, relics of the prosperous days before disease had ruined the coffee crops. Occasionally you will meet some local industry, some Heath Robinson contraption of bamboos and pipes and braziers by which the bay rum is extracted from the bay leaf. But that is all. Dominica is a poor country, though its soil is fertile; the heavy rain makes the upkeep of roads impossible. There is no way of marketing profitably the fruits that grow in profusion in the interior. It is a long, monotonous journey.

We had been travelling for seven hours. We were very sore; riding in cotton slacks when one has not ridden for many months is arduous; when, at a sudden turn of a mounting road, we saw, many feet below us, the Atlantic beating on the windward coast; half-way down the slope the red roof of a bungalow, the green flatness of a lawn, the stately dignity of the royal palm.

We were tired and we were sore and more than a little nervous as we rode up to the timbered bungalow. On the lawn there were peacocks, white and blue, spreading their vast tails. From a flagstaff the Union Jack was flying. On the verandah, in a deck chair, our host was waiting. His appearance had been described to us many times. And as he rose to welcome us he looked very much as I had expected him to look. He was tall, broad shouldered, and immensely fat. He wore a shirt that was slightly soiled and open at the neck. The belt that held his trousers had slipped, so that his shirt protruded, revealing an inch or two of skin. He wore slippers; his ankles, as he shuffled towards us, gave the impression of being swollen. He looked as I had expected him to look. A typical colonial planter. But what I had not expected was the voice with which he welcomed us. It was the courtly voice of the old-world English gentleman, with generations of breeding at the back of it.

"You have had a long journey," he said. "It is very

good of you to come all this way to see an old man. He appreciates it. You must be very tired. We will have a glass of our *vin du pays* before your bath."

The dining-room was almost entirely filled with a long table. At the head of it were laid four places. "Captain Armstrong sits upon my right. Will the elder of you sit upon my left?"

I took the place beside him. In front of each of us he set a decanter. We filled our glasses. He bowed towards each of us in turn. Then in one long sip finished the admirably mellowed rum. "And now," he said, "I will show you to your rooms."

It was a large rambling house; a bachelor's house. Its walls were lined with bookshelves and the odd assortment of pictures that bachelors at various periods of taste annex. There were hunting prints and college groups, and nudities from *La Vie Parisienne,* war-time caricatures of "Big and Little Willie." Over the washstand of each room was a printed text: "Work is the ruin of the drinking classes"; "If water rots the soles of your boots, think what it must do to your inside." A library is an autobiography. I looked carefully along his shelves. There were a certain number of novels, bought casually, a complete set of *Wisden's Cricketer's Almanac* since 1884, some legal books, the publications of the Rationalist Press, Darwin and the mid-Victorian agnostics, a few classics, a Horace and a Catallus, Thackeray and Dickens.

Dinner was ready by the time that we were. A planter's dinner. A Creole soup, a roast chicken served with Creole vegetables, boiled yam, fried plantains, sweet potatoes. But I could not believe that we were sitting at a bare deal table, in cotton and tieless suits, eating Creole food from earthenware, served by a shambling-footed negress. I felt, so completely did our host's personality dominate the atmosphere, that we were in some old English house; that the table was a polished walnut, reflecting the gleam of candles and old silver; that saddle of mutton was being served us by a silent and venerable butler; that it was Burgundy, not rum, that we were drinking.

The conversation was of the kind for which you would look in such an atmosphere. The judge did most of the talking. He was an admirable raconteur. His anecdotes were scattered with reflections. He was a staunch Tory, with little use for the philosophy and the sociology of the day. What did they want to start educating the working classes for? Education meant discontent. The working classes thought so much of themselves nowadays that they couldn't make good servants.

"And what else are they any good for?" he asked. "They're no happier now. They're less happy."

We discussed religion. He was the practical late Victorian rationalist. A Huxley, but the grandfather of Aldous, was his god.

"All this talk about heaven, as though life were a Sunday School, with prizes for the best boy. When you're dead you are dead."

The *National Review* was the only magazine he read. The old Imperial flame burnt bright in him. Let the Americans build Dreadnoughts if they wanted to, it could only mean the more for us to sink. It was thus that they talked, the English of his class thirty years back, before the war had broken finally the power and prestige of the feudal system. He typified an England that has passed.

We did not leave the table after dinner. The plates were cleared away and we sat there over our rum. The judge was a heavy drinker; every quarter of an hour or so he filled his glass, looked round the table, gave a little whistle, lifted his glass and drained it. He was a heavy drinker, but he was too well bred to put any pressure on us to drink with him. We had each our decanter at our side: we could take as much or as little as we chose. They say that wine mellows man. But I have hardly ever met a man of over forty whom wine in large quantities improves. Young people it does quite often. It removes their self-consciousness, releasing their natural gaiety and high spirits. But with older people it is more often griev-ances that are released. By the time one has come to sev-enty one has accumulated a good many unsettled scores. Now and again a peeved look came into the judge's face.

"One has to suffer for being patriotic," he said, and began to tell us some story whose details I could not clearly catch, of a naturalised German whom he had insulted in the Roseau Club. "Once a German always a German. I told him so. If I had been a younger man I should have flung him into the street. But I was fifty. They've never forgiven me down there. They all took the fellow's side."

For a moment a hard, harsh look came into his face. In an instant it had gone, replaced by the suave, courteous look of hospitality. But I could understand how that reputation for violence had grown up in Roseau. I could picture the evenings when boredom and indigestion and the tiresome company of people who would argue and contradict him would goad him, who had never borne fools lightly, into one of those outbursts that would make even his most true admirer a little frightened of him. They were few who had not felt at some time the sting of that pointed rapier.

It was after eleven when we left the table. It had been one of the best evenings that we had had since our farewell dinner to Europe in Bordeaux at the "Chapeau Rouge." But it was, nevertheless, in a puzzled, almost embarrassed way that we turned to each other the moment we were alone.

"Do you realise," said Eldred, "that he's no idea we're going away to-morrow?"

I nodded my head. Our invitation had been arranged over the telephone. Telephones in Dominica are notoriously inadequate. And during the evening several such remarks as "Captain Armstrong will take you and show you over there in a day or two," had made it very clear that we were expected to stay at least a week.

"I wish to heaven we could," I said.

Wished it both for our sake and his. There was no doubt that we should have had a delightful time there, and it was clear that he would enjoy our visit. He loved company and saw little company. It had been many months since he had seen travellers from England.

"I suppose we can't, though," said Eldred.

For a while we debated the problem. The boat on which we were booked to sail left within three days. There would not be another for a fortnight. We had arrangements to make in Martinique. We had written to friends in Barbados announcing the date of our arrival. We did not see how those plans were to be cancelled.

"It's not going to be easy telling him," I said.

It wasn't. I have enjoyed few things less than I did next morning the making of that first enquiry to the judge about the time at which we ought to start.

"Start," he said; "but where?"

"To Rosalie. I was wondering how long it would take to get there."

"But Rosalie? I do not understand."

We had exchanged half a dozen sentences before he understood.

"What!" he cried. "You are going to leave me?"

It was said on such a note of pathetic, almost childlike disappointment that I almost then and there cancelled all our Barbados plans.

"I had not realised," he said. "I thought . . ."

I began to explain. Our ship was sailing in three days. There were connections waiting. He scarcely listened. "You are going to leave me?" he repeated.

For a moment he was completely overcome by disappointment, but only for a moment. He was too good a host not to realise that a guest must not be embarrassed by a host's personal feelings.

"I am sorry," he said. "I am very sorry. But since your boat is sailing it cannot be helped. We must see about preparing you a lunch."

Immediately he had begun to make preparations for our journey. A bottle of rum was to be packed, with cheese and a loaf of bread, cold meat and fruit and pickles. He abused roundly in *patois* the servant who made up the

215

packet; but the servant laughed; his master might abuse him; but his master liked him. A negro will do anything for you provided that he knows that.

"I'll write you a letter to the overseer at my sister's property," he said. "He'll put you up for the night. He'll make you comfortable."

And he talked cheerfully as we packed of the island and the island's history, its personalities and peculiarities. But there was a wistful look on his face as he said good-bye to us.

"Come back one day," he said, "and make it soon. I won't be here much longer."

We promised that we would. We believed we would. "Within eighteen months we'll be back," we said.

When we turned at the corner of the road we saw him standing on his parapet waving his arms to us.

For quite a while we rode on in silence, picturing that long bungalow and the old man returning to his chair, his hands hanging limply over the sides, his mind abroad; thinking of what during those long hours, when the sun was too hot and he too tired to leave the cool shade of the verandah? Did his mind turn backwards to the past, to the thatched cottages of the Wiltshire where he was born, to the grey stone and green lawns of Oxford, to the mullioned windows of Lincoln's Inn? Did he relive the ardours and optimisms of youth, the tumult and the feuds of middle life, the successes and disappointments, the friendships and the enmities, the loves that went awry? Or did he, who had no faith in any immaterial heaven, look forward, adoze there in his chair, to a day imperfectly discerned when the verandah on which he sat would be

a bank of rubble, when the grass would run raggedly between the palms, when one more plantation had been re-
claimed by the jungle from which it sprang, with he himself mingled with the roots of the tall mangoes under
which by moonlight the brown people that he loved would
dance?

NEW HEBRIDES

VIII

RIGHT through the West Indies you are depressed by the sense of departed glory, and it was this feeling perhaps that made Froude, forty years ago, paint so lugubrious a picture of West Indian prospects, or it may in truth have been that at that time England was indifferent to the future of what seemed a very insignificant portion of the Empire. In so large an Empire there must always be one section whose interests are overlooked. At the moment it is the New Hebrides.

One rarely hears of them. How many averagely well-informed people in a hundred could tell you where Port Vila is? How many traffic agents in a tourist bureau would look blank if you were to ask them how to get to it? It is far away. Ten weeks from London, however you try to get there, whether you sail to Sydney and catch the *Dupleix* on one of its two monthly journeys past

Noumea; or whether you take at Marseilles one of the Messageries' cargo boats that every ten weeks or so cross the Atlantic and Pacific. Nor when you get there is it much to look at. A single row of houses, affairs of wood and tin, along one flank of a little bay. They are stores for the most part; but there is a post office, and a hotel, and a club—a bar, that is to say, where you sign for drinks instead of paying for them. There are two good houses: the British and French residencies. In half an hour you have seen all that there is to see of it. And, "If this," you say, "is the commercial centre of the New Hebrides, that's as much as I care to know about them."

Which is the attitude that the British Government appears to have adopted.

Little is known of the New Hebrides. They are off the map. No tourist boat has ever stopped there. Little has been written of them. There are a few pages in Titayna's *Mon Tour de Monde*, and there is *Isles of Illusion*, an accurate if blinkered record which had, from the point of the general public, the disadvantage of being subtitled *Letters from the South Seas*. For the South Seas is so vague a term that the book was reviewed and read, not as a picture from an angle of one section of life in the South-West Pacific, but as a general exploding of the South Sea myth. Actually, nothing could be less typically "South Sea" than the New Hebrides. You will look in vain through Santo and Malicula and Erromango for the soft hues, soft scents, soft glances of Loti's paradise. It is a harsh, hostile, fever-ridden archipelago that lies north-east of New Caledonia.

Ships carry with them the atmosphere of the countries they are bound for. Americans prefer to travel to Europe on the French Line because on the *Paris* and the *Ile de France* they feel themselves upon their beloved boulevards while they are still in Hudson River; and ten days before I had reached the Segond Channel, while I was still in the smooth waters of Sydney Harbour, I was conscious of the atmosphere that I was bound for.

Sydney is a city of contrasts. No place that I have ever been to provided me with more contradictory first impressions. It is extremely friendly, extremely hospitable. And yet you have the sensation of being an unwanted stranger. It is extremely modern, but you are conscious at every turn of history. It is extremely modern, and its hotels, by English, let alone by American standards, are mediæval. It is the seventh largest city in the world. But its inhabitants lead an outdoor country life. Every week-end they are on the beaches—Manly, Coggee Bondi—stretched out on the sand under the sun in the intervals of surf-riding. Very many of them bathe every day before going to their work. It is a city without pasty faces. No one who has been to Sydney could call Paris the city of lovely women. It is one of the chief ports of the world. Japan and China are contiguous. But there are no slums. Yet, although there are no slums, there is no city where it is more necessary after dark to keep to the main streets. Sydney is the first site for a city in the world, yet except at night Sydney Harbour is not beautiful. The rows of small houses undignify the circle of hills. I am inclined to doubt whether any modern city built on an un-American plan can be anything but petty. In mediæval days, when the peasant and artisan class were content to live in squalor, cities consisted of the few lovely buildings: the

churches, theatres, the palazzis that were the concern of
the few rich families. Nowadays, when the million demand decent living conditions, it is inevitable that the few
buildings should be obscured by the many insignificant
ones. It is in America alone that you find a style of
architecture that is adaptable to modern needs. From the
sea Sydney is not beautiful; and there are times when you
walk down its streets that you wonder whether there is an
uglier city upon earth. A moment later you are wondering if there is one lovelier. For you have turned a corner
and there in front of you and below you at the end of the
avenue of houses is the harbour, in all the beauty of its
blue distances.

> At the ends of your streets are spars,
> At the ends of your streets are stars

wrote George Sterling of San Francisco. The same words
might be written of Sydney. It is a city of contrasts. Yet
of the many contrasts that in my too short stay there it
brought me, none was more marked than my sailing from
it.

I had lunched at the "Australia." On all sides of me
young life was stirring; young life which had the harsh,
keen savour of new wine. I had driven through streets of
which fifty years earlier scarcely a stone had stood. On
Circular Quay ruffianly porters were arguing over my luggage in uncouth Australian. The Old World seemed very
far away. And then I had walked across a foot of gangway, and suddenly I was in France: in Maupassant's France,
the France of the café and the bock; of red plush couches
along a wall; of a *maître d'hôtel* venerable and pontifical

and suave. That was my first impression of the *Dupleix*, a piece of France drifted into Sydney. My second, after the bell had sounded, with the gang-plank up, the last paper streamer torn, with the Heads, jagged and menacing behind us, was still one of France, but of France setting out on an adventure.

No passenger boat—the *Dupleix* is about two thousand tons—that I had or have since travelled in possessed or has possessed so completely homogeneous an atmosphere. Every other boat has had its sprinkling of passengers travelling for pleasure, or for business unconnected with the immediate run, a sprinkling that as often as not has set the tone and pace of the ship's life. On the *Dupleix*, with the exception of a Melbourne journalist, I was the only person on board whose life and interests were not intimately bound up with the Western Pacific. It was a masculine atmosphere, almost entirely. There were one or two commercial travellers, the representatives of a Sydney firm, but for the most part they were planters from Santo, from the Banks Islands, from Erromango. Before we were through the Heads, I had the feeling of being one of a family party. Every one on the ship knew everything about each other. For a month I lived in the atmosphere of the New Hebrides. And I had the great good fortune to have as a fellow passenger the most notable personality in the West Pacific and the best *raconteur* that I have ever met, Tibby Hagen. Before we had left New Caledonia I had some idea of what I was to find awaiting me.

It was like nothing that in my dreams of the South Seas I had ever pictured. New Guinea and certain islands of the Solomon group may be more primitive. They are

223

the only parts of the world that are. The islands of the New Hebrides are mountainous; it is only along the narrow strip of beach, where the cultivation of coffee and copra is possible, that any form of civilisation exists. The bush is savage: cannibal in certain islands, and the planters are few whose bodies do not bear the scar of rifle shot and knife wound. There is always a war of some sort going on there.

"They call it a war, at least," the district officer at Santo told me. "It's more like a feud between two gangs of bootleggers in Chicago. They wait till they find one of the other side alone and then try to do him in. They're not allowed to carry arms, of course. But what's to be done? The natives who you know have rifles are usually more or less peaceable. If you disarm them, you are putting them at the mercy of the real bandits."

He took me up into the bush at Santo. The natives lived in conditions of savagery, and, as the conditions of savagery, I suspect, always are, those conditions were practical and clean. There was none of the atmosphere of squalor that you find where savage people have been forced to adopt European customs. The long huts in which they sleep, thirty or forty of them—the men and women in Santo sleep apart—are well kept and airy dormitories. They wear scarcely any clothes, which is the only healthy way of living in a hot climate of which it is said that for six months it rains and then the wet season starts. On the beach, where the missionary influence is active, the natives wear the Mother Hubbard, a garment that falls from neck to ankle. It is as unhealthy as it is unsightly. The natives wear it in the rain and let it dry on them.

When one is estimating the causes of the degeneracy of the island stock of Melanesia and Polynesia, it is hard to say who has contributed most to that degeneracy. The traders introduced rum and syphilis, the missionaries tuberculosis, those three determining maladies. It is only in the bush that you find the old stock untainted. There the women conceal only what is essential with the slenderest strip of fibre. The men consider themselves entitled to more adornment; in a cord round their waist that keeps their narrow loin cloth in position, they arrange to decorate their rumps a bunch of ferns, or if there are no ferns, feathers.

Life is simply arranged. Women work in the gardens. Each wife has a certain plot of ground that is hers to cultivate. The men do a little hunting when they feel disposed. Their pigs are their first concern. They breed or claim to breed, but anyhow possess a curious form of hermaphrodite pig which they prize highly. The pig in Santo is the gauge of income and the medium of exchange. It is with pigs that you buy your wives. You may have as many wives as you have pigs to buy them with, and here, as in Europe, it is the complaint of the young women that only the old men have the price of purchase. A good wife is worth twelve pigs. On the protruding roots of trees you will find cut the notches that are the proof of the transaction. Most of the quarrels are waged round pigs. After a year of marriage the young wife returns to her parents in revolt. The husband demands the return of his twelve pigs. The parents maintain that a year of such a consort was worth at least six pigs. The husband retorts that two is the extreme limit of her value. That in the New Hebrides is how a war begins. The district officer has to keep a record of the island feuds. He keeps it in a file marked "Pig Book."

"They never quarrel about anything else," he said; "and half the time I've not the least idea what they're fighting over. They come down here, the two disputants, and a crowd of friends. I let them chatter for a while; then when I've heard enough, I put one disputant at one end of the garden, the other at the other. Then I take the friends, settle them in the centre and say, 'Now, look here, you've got to decide this among yourselves.' I don't let them go till they've decided. After a few hours they've begun to feel hungry, and come to some compromise or other. As long as they're satisfied, I am.

"It's a queer world," he added. "Half of it's comic opera. You see that fellow over there? He's one of my policemen. Two years ago I sent him to Port Vila to serve a term of imprisonment. He came back a year later as a policeman. He liked the life apparently. And being a policeman was the nearest thing he could find to being a permanent prisoner."

Yes. There is much that is comic opera in the New Hebrides. But for the most part it is bitter earnest. The inhabitants of a country are the expression of that country, of its soil, its climate, its arid or fertile qualities. And the Melanesian, harsh, hostile and uncouth, expresses in the grim, surly set of nose and mouth the nature of the countries he inhabits. During my stay in Santo I learnt how determined is the struggle that the pioneer has to make, and the fine qualities of endurance and fortitude without which success there is impossible. When T. O. Thomas,

the planter whose guest I was there, arrived first at Hog Harbour, it was to find jungle. The plantation of forty thousand trees that stretches along the coast is the outcome of twenty years of resolute development. Foot by foot, yard by yard. It was a long struggle. The planter stands alone. He has to build his house, to recruit his labour, to plant and supervise his property. Four or five times a year one of the Messageries boats will anchor thirty miles away in the Segond Channel. Every ten weeks he will send a launch to collect his mail from the *Dupleix*. At unequal intervals some trading schooner will call to collect his copra and sell him canned goods and cotton, wine and medicines. Apart from that he is alone. He is the king and parliament of the section of country to which his plantation has brought prosperity and order. He has to maintain justice. The machinery of the law is many miles away. He is the Selfridge of his district. Most mornings you will see workmen from his plantation, "fellars belong bush," naked girls and children from the hills, gathered round his store to buy some small articles as their means afford; clothes usually— highly coloured sheets of cotton for their Mother Hubbards; food occasionally, and soap. He has to be the Harley Street as well. He has a surgery and dispensary. Without medical training, he has to deal with the tropical diseases of whose nature medical science is still ignorant. The fevers and the loathsome sores, the wounds that have gangrened with neglect. Thomas was once faced with the alternative of amputating a man's arm or letting him die of blood poisoning. He operated, and successfully. Only a man of exceptional capacities could undertake that task. Everything is against him. Nature is against him.

It is always hot and it is always raining. Nowhere have I been more pestered by mosquitoes. They arrived at dawn to vanish, curiously enough, at dusk. There was scarcely an instant of the day when three or four were not simultaneously banqueting upon me. Killing them seemed a waste of effort. Sometimes I would just watch with a weary fascination their bodies swell and redden as they sucked into my arms and knees. And yet as regards mosquitoes Hog Harbour is one of the most favoured lagoons in the group. It is fever free. And there can be few parts of the world where malaria is a more venomous foe. The malaria there is, indeed, so bad that during the war the military medical authorities would not accept any recruit from the New Hebrides.

After I had left Thomas's planation, I went round some of the islands in the *Saint André*, a seven-hundred-ton trading schooner that collected copra and sold canned goods. It was a friendly little ship. You paid your hundred francs a day passage money. It was a *vin compris* ticket. And when you arrived in the saloon for breakfast you found whisky and gin and vermouth set out ready. Every two or three hours or so it would stop at the edge of some lagoon. And the planters would come on board to arrange their sales and make their purchases. Some of them were pathetic figures. Weak-kneed, heavy-eyed, white-faced, unshaved, they would have seemed typical "white cargo" characters had you not known that only a few hours earlier they had been alternatively shivering and sweating on a bed of pain. Nature in the East Pacific is kind and cherishing; but in the Hebrides it is impossible to look on her otherwise than as on a foe. She has her beauties, inevitably; where has she not between Cancer and Capricorn? Nowhere have I seen more exquisite effects of colouring than in the lagoons of Santo. In many parts of the tropics the sands are black. But in Hog Harbour they are a dazzling white. Coral is scattered on the shore. Language has not the vocabulary with which to describe the softness, richness and variety of its blending shades. And at night, when the air is cool, when the mosquitoes are at rest, when the large moth-like butterflies flutter above the lamp in the hexagonal-shaped summerhouse, there is that utter peace which is the compensation for twelve hours' slavery. There are those sights; there are those moments. But for the most part as he rides round his plantation watching the kanakas slice open the fallen nuts, the planter cannot feel Nature to be anything but a foe.

Nor is it only Nature that is against him. The missionaries are against him. Here, as in so many other places, the missionaries use their great power with the native to persuade him that the trader and the planter are his enemy. They make trouble between the native and the planter. The native knows that the missionary will always take his side against the planter. Half the plantation difficulties may be traced to missionary influence. Nature and the missionary are against the planter. And in the case of the British planter his own government is against him, too.

In an Empire as vast as ours there must be always, I suppose, one section whose interests are ignored and shelved. Fifty years ago it was the West Indies. To-day it is the New Hebrides. Usually time rectifies neglect. To-day the interests of the West Indies are very adequately guarded. But by the time that the authorities in White-hall have realised that the New Hebrides exist, it will be too late. There will not be a British plantation left there.

The group is run by a condominium, a joint French and British rule. It should be an equitable arrangement. The French have New Caledonia as an administrative centre; the British have Australia. Most of the British planters in the West Pacific are, not unnaturally, Australians. At the moment the situation stands like this: When it is not actually impossible, it is extremely difficult for the planter to find enough local labour to work his plantation satisfactorily. The French planter remedies this difficulty by importing labour from Indo-China. This the British planter is not allowed to do. He works under an enormous disadvantage. It is only a sense of patriotism that prevents him from taking immediately the action that in many cases is ultimately forced on him, and in the future will become increasingly inevitable, that of turning his plantation into a company, in collaboration with a French shipping firm. Nominally he will hold a section of the shares; actually he will hold them all. But since the company has been registered as French he will be able to import indented labour. As a return, all the shipping of his copra will be done through French instead of British traders, and the plantation will have ceased to be British ground. In fifty years it is unlikely that there will remain a single private plantation in British hands.

It may be that it could not be otherwise, that it is impossible to make special cases with the regulation restricting indented labour. It may be that it is no great matter. The New Hebrides are few and far. I do not suppose they

are particularly profitable to any except those whose interests are directly bound up with them. One cannot,
though, be detached from the welfare of a life that one
has once been, for however brief a while, a part of; one
cannot help feeling a little sad that plantations one has
oneself seen, whose development has been achieved by one's
countrymen at the cost of so much endurance, so much
loss of health, should pass into even an ally's hands.

THE BLACK REPUBLIC

IX

THE New Hebrides are the wildest and most lawless part of the world in which I have ever been. Yet nothing could have seemed more tranquil than those green bush villages where naked savages tended their gardens and fed their pigs, in tune, seemingly, with a harmonious universe.

Which is the way with lawless places.

To-day, when I read of towns and villages taken or lost by Mexican rebels, I can scarcely believe that troops are actually deploying over the lifeless and arid plains through which I drove; that those cool villages among the hills are emptied by rifle fire; that the quiet cafés in whose shade I drowsed away the intolerable heat of a sequence of April mornings are the resort and refuge of desperate and dying men. I am not easily bored, but I was in Mexico. It seemed that nothing had happened, that nothing ever could happen there. No place seemed less potential of dramatic life.

As it was in Mexico and the New Hebrides, so was it to be in Haiti.

When I told my friends in London that I was going there they raised their eyebrows. "Haiti," they said. "But that's the place where they kill their presidents and eat their babies. You'd better buy yourself a large-sized gun."

I did not buy myself a gun. It is those who go through the world unarmed who stand the best chance of passing unmolested. But it was certainly with the feeling that drama and adventure awaited me that I saw from the deck of the *Araguaya* the blue outline of the Haitian Hills. I was familiar with Haiti's story, a long and a dark story— so long and dark that no historian can trace to its certain source the river of black merchandise that flowed during the early years of the eighteenth century to the slave factories of the Guinea coast.

For the most part it was composed, that merchandise, of the riff-raff of Western Africa; of inferior tribes that had been subjugated by their neighbours, of weaklings who had sold themselves into slavery to pay their debts. And those who judge the coloured people of the world by the negroes of the West Indies and the Southern States of America should not forget that it is from the worst elements of Africa that they have grown. For the most part, the negroes who were shipped to the New World had in their country, through their own vulnerability, degenerated into a condition of slavery. There were, however, others of a different caste: proud princes of Dahomey

236

taken in battle, in raids instigated by the slave traders—
the conditions of slavery had made highly profitable the
spoils of war—men of authority, used to the dignity and
exercise of power; men of war, fearless and skilled in
battle; the best that Africa could produce; fitted to match
a colonial civilisation that luxury and easily come by wealth
had weakened; men who were to write Haiti's history.

They were shipped, the black cargo of slaves and princes,
packed close in holds three feet in height, in which it was
impossible to sit or stand. There was no light, no air, no
sanitation. They were bound by chains that as the ship
rolled cut into their flesh. They were fed twice a day
on rice, sustained by water that as often as not was
tainted. Twice a week a ration of brandy or rum was
issued to them. Eight in every hundred died upon the
journey. During the latter half of the eighteenth century
and the early years of the nineteenth pamphlet after
pamphlet, debate after parliamentary debate expressed the
horrors of "the middle passage." But the clearest picture
of slave conditions that I have seen is to be found in a small
handbook, published in 1811, on the treatment of negro
slaves. It was written for the young planter, and was not
unlike those tips for the newly-joined subaltern that were
issued to one in the war. It consisted of practical advice.
The anonymous author regarded the negro as so much
machinery for the management of estates. His concern
was the development of that machinery to the highest
level of efficiency. One of the early chapters describes
the treatment necessary for slaves on their arrival. He
assumes as a matter of course that for days they will be un-
fit for work. They will be sick, weak, poisoned. He

catalogues the diseases from which as a result of their journey they are likely to be suffering. They will need very careful treatment. He presents his facts without comment: he accepts the conditions as a matter of course. He intends no criticism; the criticism that is implicit in that acceptance is a more potent witness than the statistics of a thousand pamphleteers.

To those who are interested in the question of the slave trade that handbook is an invaluable informant. Its argument that the slaves are the most valuable part of a plantation is usually overlooked by those who dilate on the cruelty of plantation life. A negro was worth between a hundred and a hundred and fifty pounds. One does not by wanton cruelty lessen the value of one's property. On the well-run estates the negro was happy and well cared for. He had his own hut, his own garden, whose produce he could sell, and from which he could make enough to purchase his freedom if he cared. His old age and his children were provided for. The negress would show her babies proudly to her master. "Good nigger boy to work for Massa," she would say. There were a number of suicides, but that was due to the negro's belief that when he died he would go back to Africa. In some plantations you would see cages containing severed hands and feet. This was not a warning of future punishment; it was a proof to the negro that though the gods of Africa might be able to transport to Africa the bodies of the dead, they could not transport the limbs that the white man had cut off. "Do you want," said the planter, "to go home without hands and feet? Why not wait till you die of old age and can return there complete; for I shall certainly cut off the hands and feet of every one of you that kills himself."

There were punishments, and brutal punishments, but they were used in an age of punishment, when the flogging of sailors and soldiers was regarded as a necessary piece of discipline. Examples had to be made in a country where the white man was outnumbered by the black in the proportion of ten to one. It was useless to threaten punishment. The negro cannot picture to himself the reality of pain. He lives in the minute. The negro of the Southern States enjoys the preliminaries of his lynching, the publicity, the excitement of a whole town turning out to see him. The slave who, having had one ear lopped off, was threatened with the loss of the other, fell on his knees and beseeched his master to spare him on the grounds that he would then have nowhere to put his cigarette. And it is not difficult to understand the loathsome refinements of the torture that was applied. There is no person in the world whose stupidity can exasperate you more than the negro's can.

On those occasions when every carefully repeated order has been misconstrued, when your luggage has been put on the wrong boat and the chauffeur has gone to fetch you from the wrong hotel, when you have not been called in time to catch your train and the black servant who is responsible for these misfortunes looks up at you with his incredibly stupid and lifeless face and says, "No understand," I have longed for the red-hot poker that would produce some animation in those silly features. And I can imagine how the planter, wearied with boredom and sick

with heat, must have felt under the impact of some particularly exasperating circumstance. "This slave," I can
imagine him saying, "may be worth a hundred pounds,
but my temper's worth a good deal more." They were
rich men, it must be remembered. The catalogue of punishment that Vaissière has patiently amassed would make
the Marquis de Sade envious. Such punishments, however, were exceptional. Bryan Edwards was of the opinion
that the condition of the slave in the West Indies was no
worse than that of the European peasant. Nor, though he
suggests that the avariciousness of the French made them
overwork their slaves, did he consider that the French
planters were any less considerate to their slaves than the
Spanish or English were.

Two facts, however, contributed to make San Domingo
a more likely stage for disturbance than Barbados and
Jamaica. The first that the French, though good colonists,
are never really happy out of France. The second that
the French system of the kept mistress led to a far more
rapid growth of the mulatto class in San Domingo than
in the English islands. The French never made their homes
in the West Indies. They lived in large houses, in conditions of great luxury, attended by many slaves, but their
halls were bare. They had no fine furniture, no pictures, no rich brocades. It was not worth the trouble, they
said. They were there for so short a time. Their talk
was of France; of their last visit there; of how soon they
could return. Their one object was to live in Paris on the
profits of their estates. And it was on the estate super-
vised, not by the owners, but by overseers that the atrocities were committed. It was the absentee system that was

responsible for the barbarities of West Indian life. There were many such estates in San Domingo.

There were also the mulattoes. They were rich; they had been educated in Paris; they were numerous. By the end of the eighteenth century a tenth of the French part of the island was in their hands. They had a grievance. In spite of their numbers, their riches, their education, they were allowed no voice in the government of their island. They could occupy no official position. They could get no redress from justice when they were assaulted or insulted by the *petits blancs*, the clerks and adventurers, the registrars of estates, dissolute and incompetent, whom the mulattoes knew to be their inferiors, whose acquaintance they would have derided in France, but who here could order them and outrage them because of that quartering of savage blood.

Nowhere was the colour line drawn more strictly than in colonial France. Colour precluded a man from every right of citizenship. Nowhere were the distinctions of colour defined more exactly. Moreau St. Mery has catalogued the two hundred and fifty different combinations that interbreeding may produce. The man who was four-fifths white was incontestably superior to the man who was three-quarters white. But as long as there remained a drop of coloured blood a man was debarred the rights of citizenship. The mulattoes were very conscious of their grievance. They were rich; they were educated; they were well bred; they carried in their veins the blood of the oldest families of France, of the healthiest and handsomest of the imported African. The half-caste is usually despised because he is a mixture of bad blood, of bad black

241

and of bad white. The mulattoes of San Domingo, however, combined the best of France with the best of Africa —a mixture to which most of what Haiti has achieved is due. Such men found intolerable the insults of the *petits blancs*. In Paris they were respected; why should they be despised in their own country?

Many were the complaints that they addressed to the French Government. But the French Government, blind though it was to the interests of its colonists at many points, supported them in this. "The colour line," insisted the whites, "must be maintained. We are outnumbered by the blacks in the relation of ten to one. We must uphold our prestige. We are superior to the mulatto. And by refusing to countenance the claims of the mulatto we must keep this fact before the blacks. Our prestige once lost, we should be powerless." The Government upheld its colonists.

It was, however, one of the few points in which it did. The Creole whites had grievances. In the same way that the English Government had regarded its American colonies as nothing more than a profitable source of revenue to itself, so did the bureaucrats of Paris enforce harsh and tyrannical regulations on its colonial trade. Produce might only be carried in French ships and to French ports. Duties were levied at excessive rates. The Planters grumbled. Every one was grumbling. Every one had a grievance of some sort.

Then came the revolution.

§

The story of those early months are too confused to be told in *précis*. To be understood they must be read in some such detailed study as Lothrop Stoddard's. In Paris there was a government that changed its mind only less often than it changed its leaders, that sent out commissions and recalled them, that imprisoned the colonial representatives as traitors, that one month passed an act abolishing slavery and the next repealed it. There was a society called "Les Amis des Noirs," very few of whose members had ever seen a negro, demanding the cancelling, with every distinction of class, of Moreau St. Mery's two hundred and fifty carefully compiled distinctions. There were the absent French owners, suspect as aristocrats, asserting that only on the old colour basis could the allegiance of the colonies be maintained, and Robespierre thundering back that it was better to lose a colony than a principle.

In San Domingo there were the planters, several of them aristocrats by birth, all of them aristocratic by sympathy, terrified at the thought that everything they had believed in was being taken from them, the constitution and the King of France, the tradition of colonial rule, the bar of colour. There were the bureaucrats sent out from France, ignorant, prejudiced, distrustful of every one, who sympathised with the old *régime*. There were the *petits blancs*, a worthless and crafty lot, knowing that there was nothing for them to lose, trusting that any commotion might be turned to their advantage. There were the mulattoes supporting the National Assembly, believing that at last they were to be recognised as their father's children. And there were the slaves, stupid and misinformed, vaguely aware

243

that there was an idea about that they should knock off work.

A confused and hectic story, with the planters gradually losing faith in the French Government, deciding, with the example of the American before them, on independence, appealing to the English to protect them; with Paris losing interest in its colonies; with the slaves rising and slaughtering their owners, with the mulattoes desperately appealing to the slaves to combine with them against the whites; with English troops occupying Port au Prince and the Mole St. Nicholas; and the Spanish pushing across from the west into the plain of the Gonaïves, and every man's hand against his neighbour's.

A confused and hectic story, from which emerges finally the figure of Toussaint L'Ouverture.

§

Few people have received more extravagant adulation. Certainly he was a remarkable man. A self-educated negro, he was carried by circumstances on the crest of a mounting wave. From the leadership of a band of insurgent slaves, he was swept to the generalship of an army. He drove the English out of San Domingo, annexed the Spanish section of the island, defeated the mulattoes of the south who had risen under Rigaud, in protest against black domination, and declared himself dictator. Then, with peace established in two years, he restored the island to something of its former prosperity. He returned the negroes to the plantations, and under the ruthless supervision of his generals restored a condition of industry unap-

244

proached during the days of the French planters. He was a remarkable man. But it is only the light of history falling upon him from a certain angle that has made him appear a hero.

Because he was self-educated, he has been called a genius. Because he spared the master who was kind to him he has been called human. Because he drove the English out of Haiti he has been called a patriot. Because he restored prosperity to the island he has been called a statesman. Napoleon's treatment of him has made him an object of pity. He was captured in a time of peace by treachery, shipped and left, the liberator and preserver of San Domingo, to die in a dark cell without trial in France.

That is one side of the picture. There is the other. Toussaint was the descendant of an African prince. He was born with the power to rule, with intelligence to develop his capacities. In time of revolution, for a man of force the stride is a short one from corporal to general. Toussaint was a good soldier, with the power to command. There are no signs in his character of any particular nobility. A great many negroes saved their masters. The negro is generous and remembers kindness. Toussaint was not trustworthy. He went where his interests led him. He was concerned with one thing only: the freedom of the blacks. He began by fighting for the Spaniards. Then, on realising that he would fare better with the French, he took his forces to the other side. During his long struggle with Rigaud he offered the island to the English in return for help. At the same time he was talking to the French of the "sotte credulité" of the English. Neither side trusted him. After signing peace with Leclerc, he continued to plot against the French. He had to be got out of San Domingo; and Napoleon was practical. It was as well to let die in prison those who can do you no good and may do you harm.

Toussaint was a big man. But he appears important only because he was a forerunner; because Dessalines and Christophe followed him, in the same way that Marlowe's stature is increased by being the pedestal for Shakespeare. He did little more in San Domingo than Pelage did in Guadeloupe, and had Napoleon's expedition against San Domingo succeeded as rapidly as his other one against Guadeloupe, I believe that Toussaint would have seemed as inconsiderable an historical figure as Pelage.

Nor was it on account of Toussaint that the San Domingo expedition ranks as the chief failure of Napoleon's early career.

§

Fifteen years later at St. Helena Napoleon was to describe the San Domingo expedition as a great mistake. But at the time there were reasons enough for undertaking it. The Treaty of Amiens had been signed. He was at peace with Europe. He had sixty thousand troops that he would be glad to have out of France. San Domingo had been the richest island in the New World. He had need of money. The old proprietors in Paris were beseeching him to recover their possessions. The troops who had swept so easily across Europe and Egypt could surely cope with a brigand chief. There were reasons enough for believing that the expedition would succeed. And it might have done very easily.

As easily as did his other expedition to Guadeloupe. Side by side the two expeditions were sent across the Atlantic with similar instructions. The black leaders were to be cajoled, flattered, confirmed in their ranks; then when the French army and French rule had been established the black leaders were to be returned to France; as prisoners if they had been obstinate, to serve in the French army had they been obedient. To Guadeloupe he sent Richpanse; to San Domingo his brother-in-law Leclerc, "a fellow almost damned in a fair wife."

Napoleon had planned the campaigns himself. In Guadeloupe he was to succeed immediately. Richpanse landed, paraded the coloured forces, complimented them on their courage, thanked them in the name of the Consul-General, explained that he wished them to board his ships so as to transport them further down the coast, marched them on board and into a hold, on which he closed the hatch. In a few hours Guadeloupe was his and Pelage on his way to France to serve in the French army, to die in Spain, to pass out of history.

Things went less to plan in San Domingo.

At St. Helena Napoleon was to blame himself. He was also to blame Leclerc. But the impartial historian can only reproach Leclerc with one real mistake, his attitude to Christophe, the general of the north. He might at one bold blow have taken Cap François, or he might by skilful diplomacy have overcome the black general. He delayed assault, however, and sent as an ambassador Lebrun, an ignorant, ill-bred popinjay who later, on a diplomatic visit to Jamaica, was so outrageously ill-mannered as to merit a reprimand from Nugent. It is hard to think how Leclerc could have chosen such a one as his aide-de-camp. Lebrun was handsome. Possibly he was Pauline's choice.

Christophe could have been won over. At it was, distrustful and offended by Lebrun's tactlessness, he burnt Cap François and fled into the hills. By the time that he and the other generals had surrendered into the acceptance of commissions as French generals Leclerc had lost half his men.

Even so, for the moment it looked as though the French had won. Toussaint had been shipped to France. Christophe and Dessalines were generals in the French army; according to Napoleon's plan, they, too, should have been sent back. But fighting once started is hard to stop; the hills were filled with untamed brigands. Leclerc could not risk the loss of his troops in guerilla warfare. Bandits had to be set against bandits. Christophe and Dessalines were the only men that he could trust. He had to keep them on. "A little while," he thought, "a little longer. When the last brigand has been captured, then will I send Dessalines back to France."

But the dice were loaded against Leclerc. Long before the last brigand had been brought in, yellow fever, decimating his men, had broken out along the coast, and before the epidemic was at an end the news had come from Guadeloupe that slavery had been re-established there.

It was the news from Guadeloupe that decided the San Domingan expedition, decided by uniting with a common dread not only the black but the mulatto forces. Until then the black forces of San Domingo had consisted of three armies; the mulattoes of the south, the centre under

248

Dessalines, the north under Christophe. There had been no true combination. The generals had fought and acted independently of each other. Christophe had indeed made a separate peace with Leclerc. The news that slavery was re-established in Guadeloupe, with the certainty that it was the plan of the French to restore slavery in San Domingo, united the black forces. Christophe and Dessalines went back into the hills, and with them Petion, the mulatto general who had been Dessalines' chief opponent in the early war.

For the next three years Dessalines' and San Domingo's become one story.

§

To-day Dessalines is Haiti's hero. Streets and cigarettes are christened after him. His tomb is in the Champ de l'Independence. His statue faces the Chapel of Cap Haitien. In Port au Prince it brandishes a sword in face of the green-roofed houses, the dim outline of Gonave. The visitor in Port au Prince will gaze wonderingly at that statue. He will scan the aristocratic, thin-lipped, straight-nosed face below the cockaded hat, and he will ask himself where in those bloodless features the signs of savagery are concealed. He may well ask himself. It was never for ungentle Dessalines that that mask was cut. It was ordered by a Central American president who was cast out of office before the statue could be delivered. His fall coincided with the arrival in Paris of a delegation from Haiti to commission a statue of Dessalines to celebrate the centenary of Haitian independence. As there was a statue going cheap they took it. That was the way they did

249

things in Haiti then. And, indeed, they might well have found a statue less symbolic of the tiger. As you sit at twilight on the verandah of the "Eldorado," the outline of the cockaded hat and the thin curve of the brandished sword is dark and ominous against the scarlet sunset. They are the last things you see as the swift dusk settles on the Champ du Mars.

To-day Dessalines' many brutalities are forgiven and forgotten. There was much to forget and to forgive. In Haiti's blood-stained story he is the most ruthless figure. He was a great fighter and he loved fighting. As long as he was fighting he did not much mind whom he fought. As long as he was killing he did not much mind whom he killed. In the intervals there were women. But women were a side show.

It is impossible to detect in his behaviour a consistent policy. During the two years of Toussaint's pacific administration he drove his negroes to work at the sword's point. During his war with Leclerc he butchered because they were white every Frenchman whose property lay across his line of retreat. As a general in Leclerc's army he was known as the butcher of the negroes, and slaughtered with the liveliest ferocity a hundred blacks because a few French officers had been assaulted. The war he waged with the French when the news of French treachery in Guadeloupe was known is the bloodiest in history. Terrible things happened during those weeks when Leclerc, his body faint and his eyes bright with fever, wrote despatch after desperate despatch to France, and Pauline dangled her pretty toes over the palace wall, her eye fixed broodingly on the green mangroves and the lilac outline of the hills, her ears avid for the caressing words of the young aide-de-camp beside her. Darker things were to happen after Leclerc had sunk to death, after Pauline had sailed away to a less ill-starred marriage, and the fierce Rochambeau was left in charge of the French Army. On neither side was any quarter given; no refinement of torture was left unpractised. Rochambeau imported bloodhounds from Cuba. He prepared black dummies, their stomachs stuffed with food, with which he trained the bloodhounds to make always for the bellies of the blacks. The disembowelling of prisoners was the favourite Sunday afternoon amusement of the Creoles at Cap François. Lady Nugent's journal, in the intervals of deploring the moral lapses of the young Jamaicans, makes wistful references to the atrocities that were being staged four hundred miles away. While her husband was complacently informing Lord Hobart that the French would be unable to hold out—which was to the good, he thought. "We shall have nothing to fear from the blacks," he wrote, "provided we resume our former commercial intercourse, thereby preventing them from raising a marine. There are still chiefs of Toussaint's school. We should only have to play the same game as before between Toussaint and Rigaud to succeed as well in neutralising the power of the brigands."

A few months later England and France were again at war. With the outbreak of war Rochambeau's last hope had gone. He could get no reinforcements. He could get no supplies. The blacks were attacking him by land, the English were blockading him by sea. He made peace with Dessalines and, with the honours of war, delivered himself into English hands.

It is from this moment that Dessalines appears in his full stature. Over a distance of a hundred years one reads now with a brooding wonderment the story of the next two years. Say what you will of him, Dessalines was on the heroic scale. He was of the lineage of Tamburlaine. Though his speeches and proclamations were prepared doubtless by another hand, the voice of a conqueror rings through them. Each phrase is like the roll of musketry. There is the heroic gesture, a reckless arrogance of hate, in his tearing of the white from the tricolour and making the colours of his country red and blue; in his rechristening of San Domingo; in his wiping away of the last semblance of white rule in the new name, Haiti. He let Rochambeau go on Rochambeau's own terms. He signed the papers that they brought him. He promised immunity to the white Creoles. They could go or stay as it pleased them. They would be safe. He promised. Why should he not promise if it served his purpose? A good many promises had been made in the last twenty years. Had any of them been kept? With Rochambeau safely imprisoned in Jamaica, he would decide what it was best for him to do.

He decided quickly. The French had scarcely sailed before he was thundering out his hatred of those that stayed, before he had issued orders that none of those who remained should be allowed to leave. As the weeks passed his intention grew more clear. Edward Colbert, the English representative, was writing back to Nugent that he had little hope for their safety. That Dessalines was counting his own departure as the signal for commencing the work of death. He had wanted to intercede for them with Dessalines, but "as their destruction," he wrote, "was not openly avowed by him, I was apprehensive that I might accelerate what I was anxious to avoid." He reports Dessalines' visit to the south. "In his present progress through the southern and western parts of the island he is accompanied by between three and four hundred followers, the greatest part of whom have the appearance of being extremely well qualified for every species of rapine and mischief."

Colbert had prophesied correctly. Within a week of his return to Jamaica the process of slaughter had begun. Dessalines knew that as long as there was a Frenchman left in Haiti his position would be insecure. The total extermination of the French that he had planned was a task that he could entrust to no one else. From the south, through Jeremie and Aux Cayes, he marched north to Port au Prince.

"Dessalines arrived here on Friday afternoon," records a letter found among Nugent's correspondence. "Turned loose four hundred to five hundred blood-thirsty villains on the poor defenceless inhabitants. He gave a general order for a general massacre (strangers excepted).[1] I had five in my house. It gave me great pain to be unable to save a single one of them. They were all informed against by black wenches . . . the murderers are chosen by Dessalines. They accompany him from the south to the north.

[1] In the original letter amusingly misspelt "accepted."

253

What havoc when they arrive at the Cape. The poor victims were slaughtered in the streets, in the square, on the seaside, stripped naked and carried out of the gates of Leogane and St. Joseph and thrown in heaps. A few days, I fear, will breed a pestilence. . . . Had you seen with what avidity these wretches flew at a white man you would have been astonished."

A few days later he was at the Cape. The massacre was carefully stage-managed. Guards were placed outside the house of every English and American. It was the French only who were to be killed. For a day and a night the narrow, cobbled-paved streets echoed with groans and cries. Then, suddenly, Dessalines grew weary. It was a waste of time breaking into houses, searching cupboards, dragging people from under beds. He announced that he would give safety to all whites provided that they came into the square to testify their allegiance to him. One by one the terrified creatures crept from their lairs into the open. Dessalines waited patiently beside his soldiers till the square was full. Then he tapped upon his snuff-box. It was the signal for his men to shoot.

Next day he issued the challenge of his own defence:

"Quel est ce vil Haitien si peu digne de sa regeneration qui ne croit pas avoir accompli les decrets de l'eternal en exterminant ces tigres attérés de sang. S'il un est un, qu'il s'éloigne la nature indigné de rependre de notre sein, qu'il aille cacher sa honte loin de ces lieux, l'air qu'on y respire n'est fait point pour ces organes grossier, c'est l'air pure de la liberté auguste et triumphante. . . ."

In the constitution of Haiti was drafted the proud clause:

254

"Jamais aucun Colon ni Européen ne mettra le pied sur ce terre en titre de maitre ou de proprietaire."

§

Four hundred miles away across the windward passage, Nugent, in the yellow-coloured residence in Spanish Town, addressed Dessalines, whom he described to Hobart as the brigand chief, as "Your Excellency," and in the weary well-bred indifference of official English explained the terms on which Jamaica would be ready to trade with Haiti. Nugent had no doubt of what would happen. With a tired smile he listened to the accounts that came to him of Dessalines' extravagance, of the splendour and corruption of the court, of the troops encouraged to supplement by plunder a daily ration of a herring and a half loaf. Dessalines might declare himself an emperor. But the country was on the edge of bankruptcy. Dessalines might assert that Haiti, brown and black, consisted of one brotherhood. He might offer his sister to Petion in marriage. But no declaration would convince the mulatto that he was not the superior of the negro. No declaration would persuade the negro to trust another negro. The negro could be ruled, on occasion he could rule. But he was incapable of co-operation, of rule by cabinet. When the news of Dessalines' murder was brought to Nugent— a murder, if not actually instigated, at least approved by Christophe—he was not surprised. He was not surprised six months later when history repeated itself; when the conflict of Rigaud and Toussaint, the conflict of brown and black that was to be the main issue in Haitian history

255

for the next hundred years, had been resumed between Petion and Christophe.

§

Christophe was Dessalines' second-in-command. With terror he had watched the gradual disintegration of the country under Dessalines, the disorganisation of the troops, the emptying of the treasury, the abandoned plantations. What would happen, he asked himself, when the French returned. Once the invaders had been flung back. But Leclerc had advanced on a country prosperous and prepared by Toussaint's rule. What chance would a disorganised and impoverished country stand against Napoleon? Haiti must be made powerful and rich, proud of itself, respected by other nations. Dessalines stood in the way of Haiti.

Thus Christophe argued. He had no doubt of what was needed. He had no doubt of his own power to realise those needs. When, after Dessalines' death representatives of the various departments had met to draw up new constitutions, he was so sure that that convention would place him with unlimited powers at its head that he did not trouble to attend the meeting. He remained at the Cape with the quick-brained little mulatto who was to be raised to the dignity of rank under the title Pompey Baron de Vastey, planning the details of his campaign. He was the only man in Haiti who could save Haiti; he knew that.

He had counted, however, without two things. One was his own unpopularity; a year earlier Leclerc had written home that Christophe was so hated by the blacks that there was nothing to be feared from him. On that he had not counted, nor on Petion.

§

Petion was one of the few with intellect in Haiti. He was the son of a French artist and a mulattress. He was almost white; he had spent much of his time in Paris. He had served in the French army and had studied in the military schools. He was mild and sweet-natured, with a poetic mind. He brought with him to the convention one firm resolution: that he had not driven out the French tyranny to authorise another tyranny and a black tyranny in its place.

Patiently, tactfully, diplomatically he argued clause by clause the constitution that was to defend the Haitian's liberty and limit the power of their ruler. It was no easy task. Sometimes as he looked round at that black semi-circle of surly, stupid faces, a feeling of discouragement came over him, a feeling of doubt. "This is not really what I meant," he thought. It was something quite other than this that he had planned. What was it that he had planned? He had forgotten. It was so long ago. When one was young one saw life in clear issues. Afterwards things grew confused. You fought for people with whom you were only three parts in sympathy against people to whom with a quarter of yourself you still belonged. You could never enter wholeheartedly into any quarrel. There was always a part of you left outside. Just as in life he had never anywhere been quite himself. Not here in San Domingo, where his father had been ashamed of him; nor in Paris, where they had pretended to ignore his colouring. Not even in Paris among the young officers with whom he had joked and drunk, with the woman he had loved. Always between himself and them there had been the veil of difference, this quartering of savage blood. Never anywhere had he been quite himself. That was the thing that he had dreamed of, that was the thing he had fought for, a condition of society with which man could be in tune, in which he could be himself. It was for that he was arguing now in this hot room, to these ignorant savages. It was this he dreamed of—a Utopia where man could be off his guard.

Though even as he argued, his faith weakened in the thing he argued for. They were not educated yet to democracy, these negroes. Christophe would never accept these limitations to his power. Later Christophe's indignant repudiation of the constitution came as no surprise to him. It was with no surprise that he learnt of Christophe's angry mustering of men, of his forced march over the hills into the long, sun-parched, arid plain that stretches from Ennery to St. Marc.

Without surprise, but wearily, Petion heard the news. Wearily and half-heartedly, he gathered together the remnants of the army, marched out with it into the plain, to be flung back, wrecked and scattered; himself escaping with his life and in the disguise of a peasant woman, upon the outskirts of Port au Prince. A few hours more and Christophe would be in the capital. Petion, for one last effort, gathered his strength together; with the hatred of the brown for the black, with the hatred of brain for force, with the hatred of breeding for unsponsored vigour, he mobilised his troops, marched out with them into the plain and, employing fully for the last time all that France and his father's blood had taught him, he broke and dismembered Christophe's untutored powers; broke them, scattered them; then let them go.

His generals turned to him with amazement. What, was he about to let the tyrant free? Now, when he had him in his power, when the whole of Haiti was his for the plundering! Petion shrugged his shoulders. That irresolution, that mulatto's doubting of himself that stood always between him and real greatness, mingled a little, possibly, with the poet's indifference, the poet's sense of all things' ultimate futility, made him stay his hand.

Let Christophe, he said, go north beyond the mountains; the south was safe.

So Christophe went north to crown himself a king, and Petion, in Port au Prince, drew up a constitution; a republican constitution with himself as president, and in Spanish Town, four hundred miles away, the Governor of Jamaica smiled.

§

It was less easy than Petion had imagined. He needed money to strengthen his frontier against Christophe, to prepare his defence against the French. And Rigaud had come back from France. There was a year of civil war to empty the exchequer. An exchequer that it was impossible to fill unless the people worked. They would not work if they were not driven. He lacked the heart to drive them. In his way he loved them as they loved him; the simple people who laughed so readily, who would forgive you anything provided you could make them laugh. But to be loved was not enough when you were beset by enemies.

Petion grew despondent. That doubting of himself—the mulatto's doubting of himself—and the mulatto's contempt and hatred of the black, mingled with the mulatto's envy of the white, returned to him, making it easy for him to shrug his shoulders, to let things drift. Why worry? Why fight for a liberty that its possessors could not use? Let the blacks go back to savagery. Why try to inoculate them with a sense of mission?

There was a sneer on his lips as he listened to the tales of Christophe that his spies brought to him. So Christophe was making a great man of himself up there! He had a splendid court and many palaces and counts and dukes and barons. He had a gold currency. And English admirals called on him. Professors came out from England to establish schools. The country was rich and that meant that the people of the country were enslaved. He smiled when they told him of the palace of Sans Souci. The negro's love of vanity, he called it. They told him of the citadel above Milhot, of how the people of the plains struggled to carry bronze cannon up the slope. How when the slaves paused, panting at their load, Christophe would line them up, shoot every tenth man, with the remark: "You were too many. No doubt now you are fewer you will find it easier." Of how to prove his authority he would give his troops on the citadel the order to advance and watch file after file crash over the wall to death.

Petion sneered at Christophe. What else could you expect from an illiterate nigger? How long did they imagine it would last? Tyranny had its own medicine.

He sneered, too, at the citadel. What was it, he asked, but an expression as was all else that Christophe staged up there, of the negro's inordinate self-pride? What was the use of it, after all? It would be the easiest thing in the world to surround it, to starve it out. And as for all that gold stored there in its recesses, of what use would that be there? What could it buy but ransoms? Bullion was not wealth. One day he would take his troops up there to show what it was worth.

He never did.

Petion was never to see the citadel. Never to see the sun strike yellow on its curved prow from the road to Milhot. But with the mind's clearer eye, the poet's eye, he saw it, and seeing it foresaw how that proud ship of stone would outlive the purpose it was built for, the imperial idea that it enthroned; would stand, derelict through the decades, to outlive ultimately even the quarrel so eternal seeming of brown and black.

§

To-day those pages of Vandercook's that describe all that Christophe achieved within his brief fourteen years of power read like fairy tale. You cannot believe that *Black Majesty* is history, that one man, and at that a negro, could in so short a time have done so much. You have to go to the Cape itself to realise that.

Milhot, from Cap Haitien, is a half-hour's drive. It is a bad road through a green and lovely wilderness. You can scarcely believe that this bumpy track was once an even carriage drive, that these untended fields were orderly with care, that the crumbling stone gateways, half buried in the hedge, opened on carefully-kept lawns, on verandahed houses, on aqueducts and sugar mills. Along the road passes an unending stream of women carrying, some of them on their heads, some of them on donkeys, bags of charcoal and sticks of sugar cane to market. They move slowly. The sun is hot. There is no hurry.

Milhot was once a pretty suburb of Cap François. It is now a collection of squat white-plastered houses, the majority of them with cone-shaped corrugated iron roofs; looking down on them from the hills they seem like the bell tents of a military encampment. Nothing remains of the old Milhot except the ruins of Christophe's palace. And of that only the façade and the terraces are left. Goats and lizards drowse under the trees where the King delivered judgment. The underground passage to La Ferrière is blocked. The outhouse walls are creeper covered.

At Milhot, at the police station, there will be mules or ponies waiting for you. Christophe's carriage drive to the citadel is little more than a mountain path. It is a hard two and a half hours' climb. You pass little along the way; a thatch-roofed hut or two from whose doors natives will run out in the hope of selling you bananas; a gendarme returning from the citadel to duty; a negro collecting coconuts. For a hundred years that road had been abandoned. The natives were frightened of the citadel. It was a symbol of tyranny. They could not be prevailed upon to go there. As the road mounts you have a feeling of Nature returning into possession of its own. The lizards

are large and green that dart across the road, the butterflies brighter and more numerous, the birds that dip into
a richer foliage are wider-winged. For ninety minutes you
climb in silence. Then suddenly, at a bend of the road,
you see high above you the citadel's red-rusted prow.

Words cannot describe the citadel. In photographs it
would look like any other ruin. A cinematograph, worked
from a circling aeroplane, would give no more than an
impression of it. To appreciate its meaning you have to
come to it as they that built it came to it, with the hot sun
upon you, with your back damp against your shirt, with
the fatigue of riding in your knees, with the infinitely
varied landscape before your eyes, with the innumerable
jungle sounds in your ears, and in your nostrils the innumerable jungle scents. Then you can walk along the
grass-grown courtyards, the galleries with their guns that
will never fire, the battlements through whose windows
trees are sprouting; then you can realise the prodigious
effort that the citadel's building cost; you realise that
nothing that has been said of it has been an exaggeration,
that it is the most remarkable monument in the modern
world.

§

Petion was envious. But Petion was right. It could not
last. As the months passed Christophe's tyrannies grew
more barbaric. He trusted no one. He, in his time, had
betrayed every one that he had served. Toussaint, when
he had made his truce separately with Leclerc. Leclerc,
when he had joined with Dessalines. Dessalines, whose
murder he had plotted. What reason had he to believe

that in just that way Marmelade and the rest were not plotting against him in his turn. His cruelties increased with his suspicions.

But the story of those last days has been already too well told to need retelling here. In Vandercook's pages are recounted all that can be known of the tragic drama of those last hours, of the trigger of the silver bullet pulled at length, of the mulattoes of the south sweeping victoriously across the plain. There was to be an end of tyranny. It was peace that had been fought for, it was peace that was desired. If France wanted her six million pounds as a compensation for taken property, as a guarantee of non-interference, as a recognition of Haiti independence, then let her have them. Let Haiti be free and unfettered to rule itself.

Twenty years after the surrender of Rochambeau to the English peace was signed. For ninety years Haiti was left to govern herself without white interference, and to those who claim that the coloured races are as highly developed as the white, are as capable of orderly self-government as the white, Haiti is the answer.

§

Bryan Edwards, writing of the Caribs in the Leeward Islands, made this prophecy of San Domingo. "What they are now," he wrote, "the freed negroes of San Domingo will hereafter be: savages in the midst of society—without peace, security, agriculture or property, ignorant of the duties of life and unacquainted with all the soft endearing relations which render it desirable; averse to labour, though frequently perishing of want: suspicious of each other and towards the rest of mankind: revengeful and faithless: remorseless and bloody-minded: pretending to be free while groaning beneath the capricious despotism of their chiefs and feeling all the miseries of servitude without the benefit of subordination."

In 1830 Edwards was chastised severely by the *Quarterly Review* for this prophecy. Forty years later, in part anyhow, it had been fulfilled. Politically the story of Haiti is one of tyranny and mismanagement. Of the twenty-four presidents who held office, two were murdered, one committed suicide, two died in office, two only retired into civilian life; the remaining seventeen, with as much of the national treasury as they could lay hands on, fled to Jamaica. In 1907, when Kingston was badly mauled by an earthquake, the Haitians very generously despatched a shipload of provisions for the destitute, with a naïve letter saying how happy they were to be able to do something for an island that had shown so much hospitality to those of their own countrymen to whom chance had been capricious.

The object of the majority of presidents—though there were exceptions like Hippolyte—was to transfer as much of the national revenue as they could to their pockets while the going was still good. "Graft," an English *chargé d'affaires* wrote in his report to the Colonial Office, "is the chief national pastime of the country." In such circumstances, it is not surprising that the country slipped back into disorder. Houses and roads crumbled away. "God had spoilt the roads," said the Haitians; "God would mend them."

There was no organised industry. Nearly all the land was in the hands of peasant proprietors. Coffee, which grew wild over the hills, was the chief export. When the wind blew down the pods the natives gathered them, put them on their heads or on their donkeys and carried them down to a middle-man, through whom, by various stages of bribery, they reached the Customs shed. No rich families needed to be supported from the land. All that the land was required to do was to provide in export tax enough to support the expenses of Government. That it was perfectly capable of doing so has been proved during the American occupation. It could not be expected to stand the strain of revolution, changing presidents and corrupt officials.

Life in Haiti must, during those years, have been half comic opera and half grim tragedy. During Spencer St. John's residency as *chargé d'affaires* it had an army consisting of six thousand generals, seven thousand regimental officers, and six thousand other ranks. There was little discipline. The sentries had chairs to sit upon. Justice was casual. No prisoner had any right to be considered innocent. The policeman's idea of arresting a man was to hit him into unconsciousness with a *cocomacoque,* a large iron-studded cane. Ordinarily the negro, who has a great imitative capacity and therefore a sense of precedent, makes an extremely good lawyer. But as judges were in Haiti appointed for political purposes, instances would arise in court when, it being a case of one witness's word against another's, the judge would turn with a puzzled look towards the prisoner who was accused of theft with no other testimony than the evidence of plaintiff, "But she says she saw you steal her purse. You can't get away from that, you know." Inevitably, as the money destined for public works passed into private possession, the state of the towns grew fearful. There was no sanitation. It was maintained that the harbour of Port au Prince was half-choked with filth which could be smelt seven miles out at sea.

On the surface Bryan Edwards' prophecy was being proved correct. And the surface is about all that the majority of people who wrote of Haiti at the end of the nineteenth century ever saw of it. Like Froude, they read Spencer St. John's book, and landed in transit for a few hours in Jacmel or Port au Prince. Very often captains would not allow passengers to land. Haiti to the West Indian of that time was rather what the Russia of to-day is to the European. The Jamaicans were so desperately afraid that the negroes of their island would follow the example of the Haitian that they leapt at any opportunity of exaggerating the condition of Port au Prince.

Very few of the visitors to Haiti stayed longer than their ship was anchored in the harbour. They never, that is to say, went into the country and saw the natives, nor did they in Port au Prince see anything of the Haitians themselves. Had they done so they would have learnt two things. They would have learnt that the peasant negro under conditions of freedom is a far pleasanter person than he is in slavery; and that the educated negro, under conditions where he is not presented at every moment with the consciousness of his race inferiority, develops qualities for which you would look in vain among the rich negroes of other islands. The Haitian peasant is a friendly and happy person, with no animosity to the whites, with whom you can talk as freely as you would in Sussex with an English farmer. When it comes on to rain you can take shelter in his cabin and there will be no feeling of self-consciousness on either side. While in the towns there is a society of Haitians, the majority of whom have been educated in Paris, speaking a pure French, talented and cultured, with gracious manners and a gracious way of life. Haiti has produced its poets. I do not say that they are major poets, though Oswald Durand is unlikely to be forgotten, but the existence of poetry in a society is the proof of culture. I do not see how any one who has been brought into touch with the Haitians on friendly terms can have failed to feel them to be superior to the negroes of the other West Indian islands.

No one deplored more than the Haitians themselves the anarchy into which their country degenerated during the last twenty years of its independence. It was like a wheel going down hill: nothing could stop it. The country grew yearly nearer bankruptcy. Revolution followed revolution. No property was safe when the Presidents were giving the order to their troops: "Mes enfants, pilley en bon ordre." The men in the country did not dare to come into the towns for fear of being conscripted into the army. The women who brought their produce into market were robbed by soldiers. The hills were infested by brigands. The public departments drew up schemes of development, but before these schemes could be carried out a new Government and a new set of officials were in control. As bankruptcy drew closer the certainty of white intervention grew more clear. Most of the securities of

268

the country were pledged outside the country. America was only waiting for a convenient pretext. It came during the first year of the war when, with brigands' fires burning in the Champ de Mars, and after two hundred of the most influential Haitians had been slaughtered in jail without a trial, the body of the president was torn limb from limb by a maddened mob.

§

It is fourteen years since the American marines landed in Port au Prince, and during these years a good many writers have been to Haiti. Haiti has become news. There have been revelations about voodooism, and revelations about Congo dances, and it was, I suppose, in a mood of rather prurient curiosity that I sailed from Kingston on the *Araguaya*. I do not know quite what I had expected to find there: the primitive to the *n*th degree, I fancy, and I have little doubt that any one who took the trouble to make friends with the peasants could contrive to be initiated into some lively ritual. I am not sure that it was not with some such intention that I myself set out there. I had not been ashore five minutes before I had abandoned it. There is so much in Haiti that is more worth while.

I am not sure that I had not abandoned that intention before I had even landed. Port au Prince, as you approach it, is the loveliest town in the New World that I have seen. It is white and green. The walls of houses and the twin spires of the cathedral gleam brightly through and above deep banks of foliage. The circling hills above them are many-shaded. It is through wide, clean streets, through

269

the open park of the Champ de Mars, through a town that is half a garden, that you drive out towards the hills. It is a wild, untended garden. The houses that are set back from the road are wooden, two-storied, turreted, half buried in the trees that shelter them. The roads linking the main streets are country lanes, rambling through shadowed hedges. You feel you are in an enchanted wilderness. There is nothing sinister. It is clean and fresh and green. It is everything that you expected it not to be.

There are slums in Port au Prince. Where are there not? Squalid successions of dust-covered cabins by the cockpits along the shore and on the road to Bizotin; shacks that can give you some idea of what the town must have been like before the American occupation. Once it was the dirtiest town in the Antilles; now it is one of the most attractive.

The Americans have done much for Haiti. They have cleared and laid out streets. They have made roads. They have built fine buildings. They have established hospitals. They have established order. They have wiped out the brigand forces. The men of the hills have no fear now when they come into the towns of being conscripted into revolutionary armies. The women know that they will receive in the market what their merchandise is worth. They will not have to pay toll to sentries along the way. Planters can breed cattle without the fear that they will be plundered by the *cacos*. And all this has been done with the surplus from the Haitian revenue, with the money that was before squandered in bribery. Haiti has become one of the most pleasant tropical places in the world. No island could be lovelier. Whether you are driving along the shore towards St. Marc or southwards to Aux Cayes, or whether you are climbing on horseback the hills beyond Petionville and Kenscott, whether you are looking across blue water to lilac-coloured hills or looking down upon green valleys, you will be unable to find any parallel for that landscape. The climate is healthy; the healthiest in the Antilles, doctors say. There is plenty to do. There is reasonable bathing. There are horseback trips into the interior. There is the choice for the athlete of tennis, polo, cricket. The atmosphere of Haiti is a combination of three things. There is the haphazard South Sea atmosphere of a simple, unexploited peasantry living on its own land, working just so much as it needs to support life; where there is no need to work hard if your needs are simple. They are a happy and sweet-natured people. You feel happiness as you ride past their villages, as you pass them and are passed by them on the road. Where the streams run down into the valleys you will find them in groups of six or seven seated washing their clothes upon the stones; where the streams deepen to a pool you will see them bathing, their black, naked bodies glistening in the sun. Every few miles or so along the road you will see a woman with a tray and a few bottles, a wayside restaurant, where the women will lower their loads from their heads or dismount their mules and exchange the gossip of the hour. And always they will smile friendlily at you as you pass.

There is a beauty in their little properties that you do not find in the mathematically laid out plantations. Stalks of sugar cane, cocoa trees and coffee shrubs trail side by side with mangoes and bananas. You feel here the rich luxuriousness of tropic growth as you will never feel it in Trinidad and Martinique. You feel that life is rich and life is easy. That there is no need to worry much.

You will get the same feeling if you choose as your hotel the wooden, two-storied house half way up the hills to the American Club that was the house in earlier years of a French admiral. There is a long drive leading to the house, a drive that is grass-grown now. Nor is there any fountain playing in the large stone basin. Nor can you tell where lawn and hedge divide. But the proportions of the house remain. The wide balconies, the spacious court-yard, the cameoed picture through the trees of Port au Prince. The rooms are cool and the cooking good. You never quite see how things run themselves, for there never seem to be any servants. And in the bar you will find the visitors at the hotel mixing their drinks in such proportions as they choose; but things do run themselves. Meals arrive, hot water arrives; in the end somebody signs for drinks. At the end of the month a bunch of chits arrives, and you have a pleasing sense of life crumbling round you like the garden and house; but that it will last your time.

There is the South Sea atmosphere. There is also the French atmosphere; a Parisian atmosphere of *cafés* and elegance and well-dressed women. There is more grace of living, more culture in Port au Prince than anywhere else in the Antilles. As you sit on the verandah of the *cafés* in Port au Prince, or walk on the hills in Petionville, with its little green square in front of you, its church and *gendarmerie* and playing children, you feel that you might be in the heart of France.

Thirdly, there is America: the America of efficiency, and wide streets, and motor cars, and the feeling that always goes with them, that good though the past was, the best's ahead of us.

These three atmospheres are combined in Haiti, and when there is so much else to have, it seems a waste of time to set oneself the task of discovering the ritual of a religion that is based upon nothing but the superstitions of undeveloped minds.

§

At the moment Haiti is one of the world's pleasant places. No one can tell what the future holds for it. In 1936 the American treaty with Haiti will be reconsidered, and many assert that then the American occupation should end. In America, the same kind of person who in London asserts that the English should evacuate Egypt and hand back India to its princes, is claiming that America's interests in Haiti are an imperialistic violation of the Monroe Doctrine. While many Haitians contend that America has served its purpose: it has restored order, placed a balance in the Treasury; that it has started the machine, that the Haitians can now carry it on themselves. Having learnt their lesson, they will be capable of administration; that if they are left with, at the most, a financial adviser they will be able to run their show.

They may be able to. It may be that they will be given the chance, that in six years time there will be no khaki uniforms and broad-brimmed hats in Port au Prince. That once again a negro people will be allowed to make the experiment of self-government.

And then . . . will history repeat itself? Will the *cacos* return to the hills? Will the road across the arid valley of Gonaïves crumble into a bridle path? Will the bridges justify the old complaint that it was safer to go round than over them? Will the peasant be afraid to come down into Port au Prince? Will the green lawns of the Champ de Mars straggle on to the puddled and untended roads? Will angry mobs shriek for vengeance outside the white palace of the president? Will the police with the *cocomacoque* batter the skulls of the suspected?

Sometimes one feels that Haiti is set surely now on the high road to prosperity. What else can you feel when you sit at twilight on the verandah of the Eldorado Café, looking on to the harbour, in which are anchored the ships whose presence there mean riches, when Buicks and Pontiacs are sweeping with their broad beams the broad, smooth roads and the white buildings and the pretty women? Everything looks so secure, so confident, far too far down the road of civilisation for anarchy. You think that then.

But you recall the hot and dusty mornings in the cockpit, where you have seen negroes taking into their mouths the torn and bleeding heads of the dying cock, to suck and lick the wounds, in the desperate hope of restoring the will to battle to the beaten beast. You remember into what paroxysms of rapture and misery and wrath you have seen those black faces contorted as the chances of victory recede. You remember the hot-blooded passion of their dancing, their contorted bodies, their clutching fingers, the fierce lustre in their eyes, and, remembering that, you wonder into what frenzies of savagery this people

274

might not still be worked. You remember how late at night, after the sounds of Port au Prince are still, you have heard in the hills the slow throbbing of the drums. It breaks the silence. It is slow, rhythmic, monotonous. It is like the beating of a heart, the beating of the black heart of Africa.

HOMEWARDS

X

Boat days are of too regular occurrence in Fort de France to be the carnivals that they are in Papeete. But, even so, they are gay enough in the late days of spring when a French boat is sailing for St. Nazaire or Havre. All those that can afford to are flying from the parched heat of summer. On the *Pellerin* there was not a cabin vacant. The decks were crowded. The noise from the smoking-room grew denser as *coupe* after *coupe* was drained. But I was tired; too tired to join wholeheartedly in the revelry.

It was only ten days since Eldred Curwen and I had driven from Port au Prince at four o'clock on a late April morning. But those ten days, probably because they had come at the end of five months of travelling, had been intolerably exhausting. To begin with, there had been the long twelve hours' drive across the Haitian frontier into

San Domingo, with the sun beating down through the thin canvas of the hood; there had been the heat and noise of San Domingo; the journey on that neatest of small boats, the *Antilles*, past Porto Rico; past St. Martin and St. Barthélmey, those two forgotten little islands, only touched at by one boat once a month, half Dutch, half French and speaking English: where cows and bullocks swim out at the edges of canoes towards the ship, to be drawn up by the horns on to the deck for shipment to Guadeloupe. Strange little islands. The arrival of the boat is the one incident in the life of a community which has no cars, nor cinemas, nor newspapers, nor news. The whole island puts on its smartest frocks, rows out to the ship for its three hours' sojourn, to dance in the small saloon, to be stood liqueurs, to be photographed, to take and leave addresses, then when the syren goes to scamper back into their canoes for four more uneventful weeks.

After St. Barthélmey there was Guadeloupe. The hurried rush at Basse Terre to bathe in the hot springs at Dolé; at Pointe à Pitre a casual investigation of the cyclone's damage, and afterwards there was four days of the noise and heat of Fort de France. I was very weary when the time came to move my luggage from the "Hotel Bedait" to the boat, so weary that I stayed in my cabin unpacking slowly while the syrens went and the gongs were beaten along the passage. It was not till I could feel the vibration of the engines that I came on deck.

It was a coloured scene. In the background the *charbonnières*, black and weary, chattered together behind the stacks of coal. Between them and the water half the population of the town was gathered to wave farewell to friends and relations. The Frenchmen in their helmets and white suits, the coloured people in their bright print dresses, the negroes with their handkerchiefs tied in their hair. And hands were being waved and messages shouted, and the conventional familiar thought came to me: What did it mean, this parting? What was behind those waved hands and shouted messages? Relief, excitement, sadness; to every one it must have a different meaning. Some heart must be breaking down there on the quay. And I felt sad and stood apart as the ship swung away from the docks, past the fort, into the Caribbean.

§

It was after six; in two more minutes the sun would have sunk into the sea. And it would be against a sky of yellow hyacinth that Belmont, leaning against the verandah of the little bungalow, would see the lighted ship pass by on its way to Pointe à Pitre. Through the dusk I tried to distinguish the various landmarks along the road: the white church of Case Navire, the palm trees of Carbet, the fishing tackle of Fond Lahaye. It was too dark. Martinique was a green shadow.

A few minutes more and the sun would have set into the sea; already it had set in the London that I was bound for. In the suburbs people would be mixing themselves a nightcap. In Piccadilly the last act of the theatres would have just begun. At the dinner parties that preceded dances there would be a gathering of wraps and coats. But westward, in the coloured countries, it would be shining still; pouring in the full radiance of early

279

summer over the Golden Gate; streaming southwards a hundred miles or so through the open windows of a Spanish colonial house, onto a long, low room with circled roof, onto black Chesterfields, onto a black-and-white squared carpet, onto blue Chinese porcelain, onto walls bright with the colouring of old Spanish maps. Lunch would just be over. The room would be filled with talk, with talk of plans, of golf or tennis, or a driving under the pines along the rugged Californian coast. There would be laughter there and hospitality and friendship; a bigness and an openness of heart.

And westward and southward under that same sun Papeete would be drowsing away its hour of siesta. There would be shutters over the windows of the stores; the Mariposa Café would be empty. On the balcony of the club the Chinese waiter would be lying forward across a table, his head on his arms, asleep. The water of the lagoon would be like glass; in the districts there would be silence on the green verandahs.

And westward and southward, further beyond the Heads through a mist, daylight would be filtering faintly over Sydney. There would be a chill in the air, the young women would be hurrying quickly to their shops and offices, the old men would be pulling their scarves tightly round their throats. While westward and northward, down the long, narrow peninsula of Malay, a new day would be beginning. In Penang silent-footed boys would be preparing *chota hazri*; the tea, the bread, the fruit. On the verandahs of the plantation bungalows young planters would be rubbing their eyes sleepily, looking down on the straight rows of rubber trees; at the white line of sap along the bark; at the Tamils moving quickly from cup to cup. At Lumut the district officer of the Dindings would be sitting on his balcony looking out over the brown river and the hills, fresh and friendly in the clear morning light. And in all these places, in Malaya and Monterey, in Sydney and Tahiti, I have left something of myself, so that it was only a part of myself that was travelling back to London. For that is one of the penalties of travel; that nowhere can one feel oneself complete.

And leaning against the taffrail of the *Pellerin*, watching the green dusk deepen over Martinique, I asked myself what exactly it is that one gets from travel. What stands on the credit to weigh against the debit balance? For looking back over the six months that had passed since I sailed from Plymouth, a characteristic six months in a traveller's diary, it was idle to pretend that there was not a debit or at least an absence of credit entries.

Among the letters that I had found waiting for me at Martinique were two from Inez Holden.

One bore the vast blue embossment of the Ambassador Hotel, New York.

"I have just arrived here," it ran, "which is even more strange than it may seem at first, since my departure was arranged at midnight at the Embassy Club, which is, after all, the American manner of travelling. And nothing kills one's enthusiasm more than long preparations. . . ."

She had done this, she was planning that. She had met this and the other person.

"The old policeman moving-on stunt is the order of every day. No sooner is one in Palm Beach than it is time to be on Long Island. Once there, it is time to go on to Europe. . . .

"I return on the *Berengaria* in ten days. I hope by then to be improved, modernised and dollar-dotty."

The second letter was from Berlin.

"We are here," it said, "as the guests of Otto Kahn . . . the advent of the talkies has subdued life considerably. We went round the U.F.A. studios, to find the usual scrambling, shouting, megaphone madness missing."

There was an account of trips to Wansee in a speed-boat, of interviews on reparations, of gloomy Russians "spy-shy and furtive, glancing over their shoulders nervously."

And as I had read those letters I could not help feeling that Inez Holden's life had been more full than mine had been, during the six months that had passed, since we had said good-bye to one another at the small farewell dinner I had given on my last evening in London at the Gargoyle Club. For six months I had been out of touch with the main currents. I had read no newspapers. I had seen no plays. I had been spared experience as Bloomsbury and Greenwich Village understand the term. Nor would boyhood account as experience those arguments with porters, those races down rough and winding roads, with the last syren of the steamer sounding; such dangerless discomforts as drenchings far from home and the pitch and roll of a canoe when the sea is choppy that comprise the sum of adventure for the modern traveller. There had been the seeing of lovely places. But I do not think that it is through any conscious seeking of accepted beauties that you come across those moments of sheer rapture that leave life permanently enriched. We cannot come fresh to the places in whose service the pens of innumerable poets have been held in trust. We are too much on our guard. It may be, though, that as you return from a morning at Pompeii, interested but unthrilled, to loiter for an hour or two through the streets of Naples, a chance turning your head will bring you one of those moments whose beauty is so complete that it seems possessed of eternal properties.

Of itself the thing is nothing. A long, narrow, climbing street with tall houses and green-hung balconies, lit and shadowed by a shaft of sunlight. Before one of the doorways there is an old man sleeping. A girl sings as she sews. In the gutter a child is playing. It is nothing, it is everything. By some happy accident of light and grouping this ordinary, familiar street has been lifted out of time and space to partake of an immortal quality. It is sheer effect. Five minutes before it was not. In five minutes' time it will have passed. The sun will have moved westward, the girl will have ceased to sing. The old man will be awake, the child in tears. Such moments are imperishable and fleeting. And one is as likely to meet them in Tooting as in Tangiers. I do not expect ever to see anything lovelier than Constantinople. There are places where beauty is achieved by Nature in spite of man, and others by man in spite of Nature, but once in many times Nature and man combine to create something that is beyond beauty, that transcends the power of pen and brush. At first I could not believe that it was real. From a distance it may be lovely enough, I thought, but seen from this or that other spot the details will grow distinct.

There will be mean houses and dingy streets. I shall see it for the thing it is. But the boat drew closer. One by one against a saffron-coloured sky the buildings grew separate and clear, the low sea wall, the Doric columns, the round morgue, the dignity of San Sofia. Slowly the boat swung round into the harbour, and there it lay, the city that was loved of Loti, a far-flung crescent, aureoled in a faint haze of smoke with the sunlight pouring down the Corne d'Or, on to that exquisitely proportioned line of mosque and minaret. "Rose of cities," was Flecker's phrase for it, and there is a flowerlike quality in its effortless perfection, a flowerlike bloom on the golden mist that hovers over it.

I never expect to see anything lovelier. But the thrill with which I looked at it from the steamer's deck was no greater than the thrill with which at certain moments I have seen London in rain and sunlight. Nor, were I to return to Constantinople, should I find the same city waiting for me. It was the moment that made it beautiful. Once when I was crossing the bridge over the lake in St. James' Park, I thought that Whitehall, through the lilac mist of a November afternoon, was an enchanted city out of the *Arabian Nights*. I have sought often for that city since, and have never found it. During my six months in the West Indies I had seen many lovely places. But I think I should have had just as many moments of surprised delight had I stayed in London. The sight-seeing part of travel scarcely compensates for the expense of spirit that seeing them involves.

There are pictures enough for the wanderer to bear home with him. But it is not these that are the rewards of travel. It is not these that every morning make one read enviously through the list of mails and shipping; that whenever one hears of a ship sailing make one long to sail with it. It is not for these one travels.

The charm of travel, as of most things for that matter, is, I think, something intrinsic to itself, to be pursued as that of art for its own sake. It is not so much the places you visit as the getting there, not the end but the means that matters. In the very sailing of a liner there is a thrill for which life has no equivalent. It is its very absence of drama that is so dramatic.

You are at a dinner party in New York. Eleven o'clock has passed. Watches are being glanced at. "Are you coming on to the Wellingtons'?" some one asks. You shake your head. "I'm sorry," you say, "I sail to-night." "Really," your hostess answers, "then you'll be able to see Miss Gathers home." And as you drive westward in the taxi, you chatter of mutual acquaintances and the party you have come from. And it is all a little shadowy, like a blurred film. You cannot believe that it is quite real, this party and this talk of parties. It is a world that exists, that will go on existing, but that in a day's time will have ceased to exist for you. In half an hour you will be on a ship. And yet you cannot believe that you are really sailing, that at last the long-awaited adventure has begun. You had expected it to be different. You cannot even believe it when you are in your state-room, when the steward is unpacking your trunk. You look incredulously at the porthole. Is it really through that circle of glass that you are to see the swaying palm trees and the golden sands of the West Indies?

Or, maybe, it is from Marseilles that you are sailing. You have been travelling all night by train. It was windy and wet in Paris, and the breakfast car, that is bright with sunshine, is full of people chatting excitedly about the glories of the Côte d'Azur, Cannes, Monaco, Antibes; names that are for months now to mean nothing to you; to you who are travelling ten thousand miles across the Atlantic through Panama to a green island in the Pacific.

And as you drive through the winding cobbled streets towards the docks, there is a curious contrast between the excitement you are feeling and the indifference of every one about you. There is an utter absence of all fuss. There is no commotion, no crowd upon the wharf. Your ship is just one out of a score of ships. There they are in rows, with the blackboards hung upon their gangways. *"Le Louqsor* partira à 11.30 pour Pointe à Pitre." Just that, the bare wording of a notice. And you think of all that those words convey of time and distance. While to the officials round the dock the sailing may be a matter of mere routine, to you it is the big adventure of your life. And yet there is nothing to show it is. Is this really the way, you ask yourself, that you say "Good-bye" to every one and everything that hitherto has comprised life to you? Is this the way you set out into the unknown? You had expected that such moments in your life would be accompanied by the conventionally appropriate trappings, some equivalent to the old fanfare of trumpets that heralded departure. And even as you wonder, you know that it is better so, that nowhere else could you get the acuteness of the thrill with which you hear the groan of a weighed anchor. It is a thrill only to be compared with the excitement of arrival; a thrill that is independent of the beauty and attractions of the place that you are bound for; that is great or little in accordance with the length of the journey you have made. Æsthetically, San Francisco is at its loveliest as you come to it from the Pacific, through the Golden Gate, but the first sight of it to the traveller from Honolulu will not produce the same tightening of the muscles round the heart that you get when you reach it by ferry boat from Oakland Pier, after seven days of the Atlantic and four days of train across a continent. In the same way that one's enjoyment of a meal depends on the amount of time that has elapsed since one ate one's last, so does one's excitement on reaching a new place depend on the measure of effort that one's arrival there has cost.

I shall never forget the excitement of my second arrival at Tahiti. In the course of six and a half weeks we had only stopped three times and for a few hours. For twenty days we had not seen land; if I had been told that we should have to spend another two weeks on board I should have, I think, gone mad. For days we had been watching the flag move forward on the map, calculating how long it would take to reach Papeete, wondering whether by some happy hazard of wind and current, we might not arrive ahead of time, suspecting that in all probability we should be hours late.

It all seemed worth it, though, on the day that we arrived. We were to reach Papeete shortly after one. And at half-past five I was on the bridge peering ahead through the dissolving dusk. Slowly the sky brightened; slowly the sun came out of the sea behind us. Eagerly I looked ahead. Was that a cloud there, or a line of mountains? It was so faint and shadowy. Was it really the outline of the Diadem, or just a cloud that shortly would dislimn? And when, at last, I realised that that lilac shadow was not a cloud, but was in very truth Tahiti—that moment paid and repaid the score of those long six weeks.

That is the thing about travel. It is not so much that one sees the world through it as that one comes to a whole new series of sensations that are to be won to nohow else. For, in point of actual worldliness, the sailor, though he has touched at so many corners of the world, knows little of it.

§

I have travelled, I suppose, in all on something like thirty ships, varying in size from the vast Atlantic ferry boats to the little trading steamers that coast round the lagoons of the New Hebrides; I have seen something of the sailor's life, and, however much the actual conditions governing it may change, in its essentials it remains the same.

We listen enviously at first to the sailor's account of the seas he has crossed and the lands that he has visited, but in actual fact he sees nothing of those far countries except their coastline. He rarely remains for longer than five days at any port. There is work to be done upon the ship; there is no time to go far inland. He has only a few hours at his disposal. He has no friends ashore. As likely as not the language is foreign to him. The cafés are the only places that he can go to; there is not much difference between one café and another.

"My word, but I could tell you some stories about this

place!" said once to me a certain companionable second steward, as we were strolling down the main thoroughfare of Manzanillo, that most lugubrious of all the lugubrious coffee ports which stretch along the Mexican coastline between Mazatlan and Acapulco. It is a one-street affair with a couple of cafés, a store or two, a shambling hotel, and the kind of dance place where only a fool would flash a ten-dollar bill; where every one carries a revolver on his hip, and the evening is as likely as not to end with the sound of bullets.

"I could tell you some stories about this place," said the second steward. "Seven whole weeks I spent here once."

He was a Peruvian, half-native and half-American, with a quick wit and a twinkling eye, who had spent thirty-five years coasting between Seattle and Valparaiso. He had had his share of improbable experiences. But even so the prospect of listening to his confession did not fill me with the curiosity that two years earlier it would have done. I knew in advance the details of that story.

There had been a heavy night, with a boat to sail at six; there had been drinking, there had been a quarrel. And at half-past seven he had found himself in a back alley, his pockets empty, his comrades gone, and not another ship due for seven weeks. He had reported to his Consul, who listened wearily to a wearily familiar tale, and promised him twenty-five cents a day till succour came. Then there had been a girl.

"As fine a girl, sir," he would insist, "as you would be likely to find anywhere along the Lincoln Highway. I cried my eyes out when I said good-bye to her. I swore

I'ld come back; and the things I promised to send her when we got to San Francisco! I meant to send them, I swear I did. But you know what sailors are. You go ashore with six months' pay, within six hours there's not a penny left of it; and there's nothing for you to do but to find another ship and sign on quickly."

The land life of the sailor is narrow, uninteresting, and, in the true sense of the word, unromantic. It is, however, an inessential part of the sailor's life. You can get no true picture of his real life by watching him in a "dive" in Colon, or in the chop sueys that are north of the West India Docks. He is a seaman and his life is on his ship.

At sea he is a very different person, simple and direct, leading a healthy, pleasant, monotonous existence. His life is centred in his ship and his companions; he has no part in that which constitutes the life of the normal landsman. He rarely reads a newspaper, politics mean nothing to him; his conversation is not a fabric of murder trials and football results. He is concerned with currents and cargoes; with the day's run, with the changing winds, with the infinite variety of the sea, with the interests that compose the sum of a communal and self-contained existence.

He has simplified life into two things, his ship and his home. Home does not mean to him a fabric of complicated relations, but two or three people—his parents, his wife, his children. A sailor, for all they may talk about the "wife in every port," is an extremely domesticated person. He has no opportunity of knowing more than a very few people intimately, and his life is bound up in those few. The excitement of arriving at port is more often the thrill over a mail than the prospect of an hilarious evening.

We picture the sailor's life in terms of adventure and romance. We think of the sailor as some one who has seen life widely; but in point of fact there is no class of person who is less familiar with what is held ordinarily to constitute life. In consequence, he retains that freshness, almost amounting to an innocence of outlook, that is his particular and peculiar charm.

§

And it is for this reason, I believe—namely, that the reward of travel is not the seeing of certain accepted beauties but the discovery of a series of special and particular sensations—that so many travellers will tell you that the biggest emotion that they have ever had is the crossing of the Panama Canal. The passing of those locks, that stepping in a few hours from one ocean to another, which is the stepping from a known into an unknown world, symbolises the whole spirit of adventure that lures men to travel. And here, too, there is the drama of the undramatic. There is no fuss. It is very quiet and orderly and efficient. There is no shouting, no display. The great gates close behind you; noiselessly the water fills the lock. Inch by inch you rise till the figures that were on a level with the deck are feet below it; till another gate swings open and the traction engines begin to climb; and once again there is the noiseless flow of water; and once again the figures on the side that were above you are at your level and then are passed. It is so quiet that you scarcely realise the immensity of the adventure; not even when you are in the Gatun Lake and see to right and left of you the stumps of the flooded forests; not even when you drift slowly past Miraflores towards San Miguel, towards Balboa and beyond Balboa, to the slow waters of the Pacific.

If ever I write a travel story it shall begin in Panama, with the first sighting after three weeks of the Atlantic of the breakwater of Colon. And as the boat rises slowly the hero will feel that he is being lifted out of the world of commonplace experience into the rarefied atmosphere of romance. To a love story, the return by the Canal would give the perfect curtain. As in the first chapter the approach to Colon had symbolised the spirit of romance, so now would the return through Panama symbolise its death. As the hero looks behind him at those closing gates and upwards at the heightening shore and before him to the low Atlantic, he realises in one spasm of revelation all that he is saying good-bye to. He is descending from the heights of poetic living to the prosaic level of mere livelihood.

LONDON

XI

IT is at Plymouth that the traveller should land. The cool green of its hills will mean England to him after the gaudy tropics. And it is through landscape that contains the heart of England that the train will hurry him to London. You have not the same feeling of home-coming at Southampton. Certainly you have not if you arrive there in the early morning by the night boat from Havre.

The *Pellerin* had docked early in the afternoon. Eldred had caught the special train to Paris, and as I wandered round the streets, or sat in a café reading the *Continental Daily Mail,* I had the feeling of being back and yet not back. It was an impression that persisted. On the small Channel boat there was the restlessness of interrupted travel. There was shouting and a clattering of trunks. The cabins were small—the kind of cabin that is meant to be slept no more than a night in. It was by European labels that the suitcases of the man who slept in the next bunk were covered. Next morning the familiar platform was busy with the familiar bustle: with the familiar faces draggled after a restless night and a hurried dressing. I could not believe that it was from the tropics and a six months' absence that I was returning. I felt that, like all these others, I was coming back from a week-end in Paris.

And yet, perhaps, it is in that way, anonymously, that one should return to a city so vast that one can be free in it. You can do what you like in London because no one in London has the time to wonder what you are doing. It may be that that is so also in Berlin and Paris and New York. Probably it is. I do not know them well enough to tell. But in every other place that I have ever known I have had the uncomfortable sensation of living in a glass house. One has no private life. One is under constant observation. Even in Tahiti, where one can do what one likes, everybody knows what one is doing. London is big enough to mind its own affairs. And as the train rattled through Hampshire I felt that this was the way in which one should come back: in a breakfast car surrounded by the clatter of many courses, among people who seemed to have spent the last fortnight in precisely the same way, though as likely as not the experiences of each person in that car were as diverse and varied as my own. That is, I suppose, one of the paradoxes of the English, that about the most personal and individual race in the world should give the impression of having been turned out to pattern.

294

I drove straight from Waterloo along the Embankment, up Regent Street, towards my club. The porter received me as though I had never been away. His "Good morning, sir" had its invariable intonation of respectful and indifferent welcome. The boy who took my trunks and suit-cases from the cab cast no inquisitive eye upon the labels. I walked into the club. It was a little after nine. Breakfasts were still being served. There was only one man in the reading-room. I knew him fairly well. We would exchange the conventionalities of small talk two or three times a week. And once a month or so we would sit next each other at lunch or dinner. He must have known I had been away. But he had taken as little count of it as he had of such other things as we may have heard of one another, but to which it would never have occurred to us to refer. In a London club you leave your private life with your hat and overcoat in the hall. He turned his head as I came up to him.

"Ah, Waugh," he said, "there's something I wanted to ask you. I was thinking of getting a first edition of *Avowals*. How much ought I to give for it?"

"Three guineas," I suggested, and I sat beside him, and for half an hour or so we talked of limited and first editions.

And later, after he had gone, and I had settled myself in a corner chair with a pile of newspapers beside me, it was with the same feeling of having always been there that I turned the pages of the *Tatler*. The same people were being photographed in the same company. The gossip column was filled with familiar names. The same parties,

295

the same guests. In the literary page I saw that the same authors were producing the same books with the same measure of success. Nothing had changed. I might never have been away.

§

"Does London seem very strange," I was once asked, "when you've been so long away? Does it seem smaller, when you've been so many miles from it?"

"You see it differently," I said.

Or rather, you see it against a different background. In the same way that by reading history you have a standard for the political columns of the daily newspaper, and by reading the literatures of France and Rome and Greece you have a standard for that of your own country, by travel you come to see from a different angle the stir and conflict of London. Which is not to say that London seems any the less important.

There are people who will say that London does not matter, that London is not England, that Manchester is England, that Sussex is England, but that London is not England. Though what else it is, considering the number of Englishmen who inhabit it, I have been unable to discover. The provincialism of such a contention is surely as narrow as that of those few Londoners whose world is bounded by a few streets, a few houses, a few names, to whom no one unestablished within that circle matters, whose scale of values does not recognise the existence of those huge spheres of commerce and administration which develop and safeguard the interests of the country.

Travel does not make London seem either small or strange. On the contrary, there are sides of London life whose stature is infinitely increased by travel. You cannot travel through the Antilles and Australia and Malaya without feeling how immensely important is the headpiece that directs this vast and varied Empire. For that is what London is. To London come the best brains of England, and from London go the ideas that are to control those immense tracts of land, those haphazard minglings of warring nations, those young peoples of the new world that are rising to significance. London is the administrative centre. It is hard to exaggerate the value of what that section of London that is representative of England's larger interests thinks and feels and says.

§

It is oneself chiefly that travel alters. It gives one an "otherworldliness," the kind of "otherworldliness" that at Oxford comes to one through "Greats." For it is not possible to linger among those green islands whither no newspapers ever come, where life follows its tranquil course, indifferent to what is happening in Europe and America, without wondering whether anything really matters beyond the setting of oneself in harmony with those eternal forces of birth and growth and ultimate decay that weave their gracious pattern by the palm-fringed beaches. Of this I am very sure, that whatever may lie ahead for me of success and failure, of happiness and disappointment, I shall have to counsel me against too ready a surrender to the moment's mood, the memory of that little island to which no echo of our western turmoil can ever reach.

In the same way that the shepherds recall by the site of Uricon "the Roman and his trouble," I shall remember the long curve of that little harbour with the nestling schooners and the painted bungalows, and across the lagoon the many pinnacles of its sister isle. I shall remember the gentle manners of its people, the dark-skinned Polynesians, the French officials, the Chinese traders. I shall remember their soft singing and the glimmer on the water at nightfall of the torches by which they fish. I shall remember their cool verandahs, the red and white of the hibiscus, the yellow amanda flower and the purple of the bougainvillea; I shall remember how the sun shines and the earth is fertile and nobody is sad.

And I shall know that were I to return there, I should find the same merrily laughing group drawn up along the wharf. They would know nothing of how life had fared for me in Europe. The things that make for one's reception here, the opinion of one's fellows, the sales of one's books, one's prices from the magazines, one's quarter or half column notices in the Sunday Press would count for nothing to one returning to that green island.

There would be the hailing of a remembered face. *"Ia ora na,"* they would shout to me. They would wave their hands. There would be a drifting towards the café, a laughing together over ice cream sodas. And after the sun had set, a miracle of golden lilac behind Moorea, there would be a wandering to the Chinese restaurant for a chop suey, with afterwards a riding out along the beach with the moon shining upon the palm trees, and the warm air scented with the white bloom of the tiare. There would be the singing, the laughter and the dancing, a sense of unity with primæval forces.

And ultimately that is, I suppose, what death will prove to be: a stepping away from what is transient into the waveless calm of an eternal rhythm.

AUTHOR'S NOTE

IN a travel book such as this, I feel that footnotes could only be an inconvenience to the reader. So I have let the section about Haiti stand without any quoting of authorities.

The bibliography of Haiti is not long. Any one who cares to spend a few hours in the British Museum reading room will be in a position to dispute my interpretation of those facts one can be sure of. They are not many. Vaissière's *Saint Domingue* is a scholarly study of the island's life up till 1789. But from then onwards the historian has to rely very largely upon guesswork. The documents on which accurate conclusions might be based do not exist. Lothrop Stoddard has written a careful and dramatic account of the years 1789-1803. But he has had necessarily to base his opinions on French official documents. He had no means of seeing the other side of the picture. With the surrender of Rochambeau and the massacre of the white planters, darkness descends. There is no impartial witness. The various histories of Haiti have been written by men with an axe to grind: by French colonials trying to explain their failure; by mulattoes concerned with an attempt to attribute the island's misfortunes to black mismanagement; by negroes blaming those misfortunes upon mulatto weakness; by mulatto and negro apologists who denied that there were any misfortunes to be blamed on any one; by Englishmen who were terrified lest the Jamai-

301

cans should follow the example of their neighbours; by casual tourists who accepted the testimony of the first history they picked up; by Americans who approved and Americans who opposed Washington's interference. The most balanced history is H. P. Davis' *Black Democracy*.

In the outline of Haitian history that I have sketched I have relied upon that evidence that seemed to me least partial: in particular upon the Nugent papers in the Jamaican Institute. They have not, as far as I know, been quoted from before, and my gratitude is very great to Mr. Frank Cundall and his assistants, who helped me to find a path through them. The official English in Jamaica were relatively independent and well informed. Colbert's despatches to Nugent and Nugent's to Hobart are the honest expressions of opinion of men who stood above the battle. But they are quite likely to have been mistaken. One has to accept out of one's general knowledge of the period, of the country, of negro and mulatto characteristics what appears most probable. There is, for instance, no proof that Christophe was concerned in the murder of Dessalines. I do not believe, however, that Christophe, had he been innocent, would have protested his innocence so indignantly and so self-righteously.

Throughout I have used the word "coloured" in the West Indian sense of half caste, and the word "creole" in its original sense of "born in and native to the colonies." The word has nothing to do with colour. There were black, white and mulatto creoles.

INDEX

INDEX